des Papes

NEUF-DU-PAPE
BRUNEUF-DU-PAPE CONTRÔLÉE

750 ml

Les AVRIL premiers Consuls et Trésoriers
de Châteauneuf-du-Pape de 1756 à 1790

CONTAINS SULFITES

Chablis Grand Cru
Clos
APPELLATION CHABLIS GRAND CRU CONTRÔLÉE
ALC. 13% BY VOL.   PRODUCE OF FRANCE   750 ML
Mis en bouteilles à la propriété
DOMAINE FRANÇOIS RAVENEAU À CHABLIS - FRANCE

DOMAINE
Jamet
Côte-Rôtie
Appellation Côte-Rôtie Protégée
Côte-Brune
Mise en bouteille à la propriété
Corinne, Jean-Paul & Loïc JAMET
« Le Vallin » - AMPUIS - France
13% vol.   75 cl

ALSACE GRAND CRU

MW00823904

RANGEN DE THANN
Appellation Alsace Grand Cru Contrôlée
TOKAY PINOT GRIS 1990
alc. 14% by vol   750

DOMAINE ZIND HUMBRECHT
Léonard et Olivier HUMBRECHT - WINTZENHEIM (Haut-Rhin) FRANCE
TABLE WINE - PRODUCE OF FRANCE   L 550606

Château Cheval Blanc
1947
St Émilion
Hers FOURCAUD-LAUSSAC
PROPRIÉTAIRES
Mis en bouteille au Château   (FRANCE)
APPELLATION CONTRÔLÉE

PRODUIT   DE FRANCE

Corton-Charlemagne
GRAND CRU
APPELLATION CORTON-CHARLEMAGNE CONTRÔLÉE
WHITE BURGUNDY WINE
ALC. 13% BY VOL.   J.-F. COCHE-DURY   750 ML
PROPRIÉTAIRE-VITICULTEUR A MEURSAULT (CÔTE-D'OR)
PRODUCT OF FRANCE

CHÂTEAU AUSONE
SAINT-ÉMILION
1928

Le Pin
POMEROL
APPELLATION POMEROL CONTRÔLÉE
VITICULTEUR
82
MIS EN BOUTEILLE AU CHATEAU   75 cl

CHATEAU-FIGEAC
PREMIER GRAND CRU CLASSÉ
ST ÉMILION
Bouteille N° 00000

Champagne Private Cuvée
KRUG
KRUG & Cₒ
REIMS
T BRITAIN   EXTRA

MEDOC
MARGAUX, FRANCE

Vins de   Bourgogne
CARILLON
1632
BIENVENUES-BATARD-MONTRACHET
GRAND CRU
APPELLATION BIENVENUES-BATARD-MONTRACHET CONTRÔLÉE
1990
Louis CARILLON et Fils
VITICULTEURS
PRODUCE OF FRANCE

Château-Chalon
APPELLATION CONTRÔLÉE
13.7% Vol   620
JEAN BOURDY - ARLAY - JURA - FRANCE
PRODUIT DE FRANCE

CHÂTEAU AUSONE
SAINT-ÉMILION

PRODUIT DE FRANCE
TRADE   MARK

HERMITAGE
APPELLATION HERMITAGE CONTRÔLÉE
La Chapelle
PAUL JABOULET AÎNÉ
Mis en bouteille par
PAUL JABOULET AÎNÉ 26600 - LA ROCHE DE GLUN (FRANCE)

ANÉE
EAU

ER-BELAIR
-ROMANÉE

Richebourg
Grand Cru
Appellation Contrôlée
Mis en bouteille par
Négociants à Auxey-Meursault (Côte-d'Or)

1947
BONNET ROUGE

Vouvray
APPELLATION CONTRÔLÉE
A. FOREAU
PROPRIÉTAIRE AU "CLOS NAUDIN" A VOUVRAY (I-&-L)

Mis en bouteille au Domaine
CHAMBERTIN
Grand Cru
Appellation   Contrôlée
1990
Domaine A. Rousseau P. & F.
Propriétaire
21220   Gevrey-Chambertin   France
13% vol.   Product of France   750 ml

y

Grand Cru
MONTRACHET
APPELLATION CONTRÔLÉE
S.C.E. DOMAINE RAMONET
VITICULTEUR A CHASSAGNE-MONTRACHET
CÔTE-D'OR, FRANCE
14% vol.   750 ml

PRODUCE OF FRANCE
L. MONT m.

PRODUCT OF FRANCE   CONTAINS SULFITES

MIS EN BOUTEILLE AU CHÂTEAU

CHÂTEAU RAYAS
CHATEAUNEUF-DU-PAPE
RED RHONE WINE
APPELLATION CHÂTEAUNEUF-DU-PAPE CONTRÔLÉE
Alc. 14% by Vol.
S.C.E.A.   CHATEAUNEUF-DU-PAPE
CHATEAU RAYAS   VAUCLUSE
750 ml   FRANCE
IMPORTED BY
MARTINE'S WINES INC. - NOVATO CA 94949

MONTRACHET
APPELLATION MONTRACHET CONTRÔLÉE
2.735 Bouteilles Récoltées
N°   LES ASSOCIÉS-GÉRANTS
ANNÉE 1978
Mise en bouteille au domaine
PRODUCT OF FRANCE

WINE & TRAVEL
FRANCE

To Donata and Andrea,
who have given me
the most essential things:
a passion for taste and a love of life.

TEXT BY ENRICO BERNARDO

WINE & TRAVEL
FRANCE

ASSOULINE

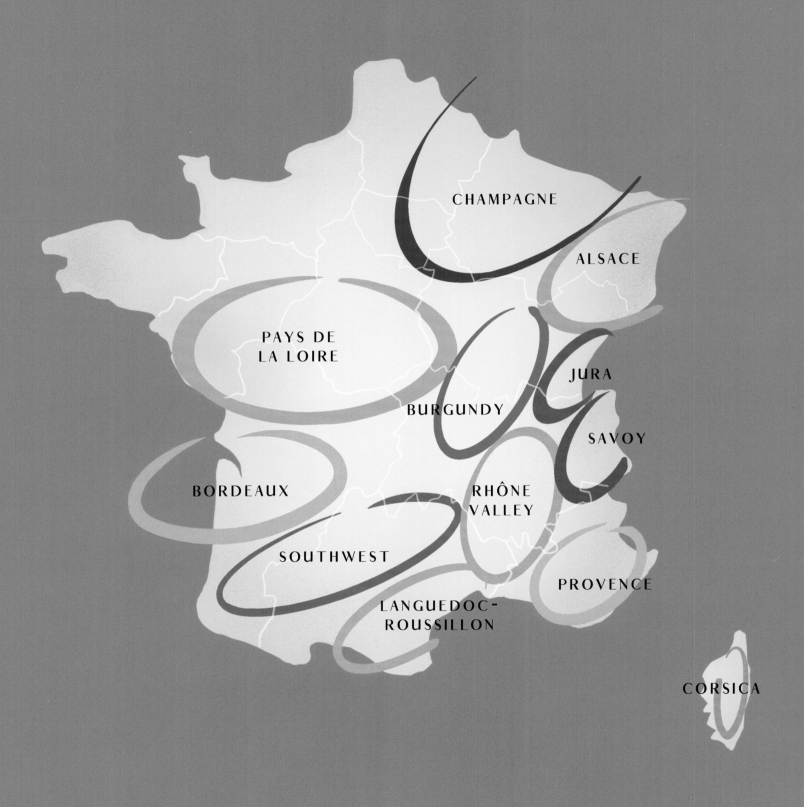

CHAMPAGNE

ALSACE

PAYS DE
LA LOIRE

JURA

BURGUNDY

SAVOY

BORDEAUX

RHÔNE
VALLEY

SOUTHWEST

PROVENCE

LANGUEDOC-
ROUSSILLON

CORSICA

THE HARVESTING REGIONS OF FRANCE

PREFACE

For thirty years I have visited the vineyards of France, where I never cease to discover innovative winemakers at work. The global wine tour that is the basis for this book, and those that will follow, will in the end take five years, of which I have already spent one whole year in France: four months in the Côte-d'Or, two in the Rhone Valley, one in Champagne, another in the Loire Valley, and then Alsace, the Jura, Roussillon, Beaujolais . . . I could go on. I have visited on average twenty to twenty-five estates per week, meaning four or five each day, and more than a thousand in total. And all that without enduring a moment's monotony: Each winemaking region has its own rhythm. When the estates lie close together, it is easy to visit them one after another. In other cases, I could sometimes see no more than three in one day. The number of wines to taste varied as well. In Bordeaux, I rarely tasted more than four wines at each chateau, which made possible six tastings per day. In Alsace, however, the situation is entirely the opposite: What with the array of varietals—Riesling, pinot gris, muscat, Gewürztraminer, Sylvaner, Pinot Noir—and a gamut that runs from entry-level wines to grands crus, and from dry wines to sélections de grains nobles, not to mention the winegrowers' generosity, tastings could take five or six hours. Anyone who has never undertaken such an exercise might find all this a bit crazy, not to mention simply exhausting. But for an unconditional wine lover like me, it's all in a day's work.

In this book, then, I invite you to come along on a journey through the twelve great wine-growing regions of France. I hope that you will encounter as many wonders along the way as I did myself. And I hope that you will join me in discovering still more on my next journeys, in the future books of this series, as we seek out new wines and the exemplary winemakers who create them.

At the end of this book, you will find a list of the most memorable wines from our tour through France. My wish is that this might become for you a dream made real, in which each bottle finds its consummate moment thanks to the dish or the specific occasion that it perfectly accompanies. Most of all, I hope that you are able to share every bottle you open with those near and dear and who appreciate it as much as you do.

Enrico Bernardo
Paris

Ian Greathead, *Premiers Crus,* 2020, oil on canvas, 76.2 x 101.6 cm.

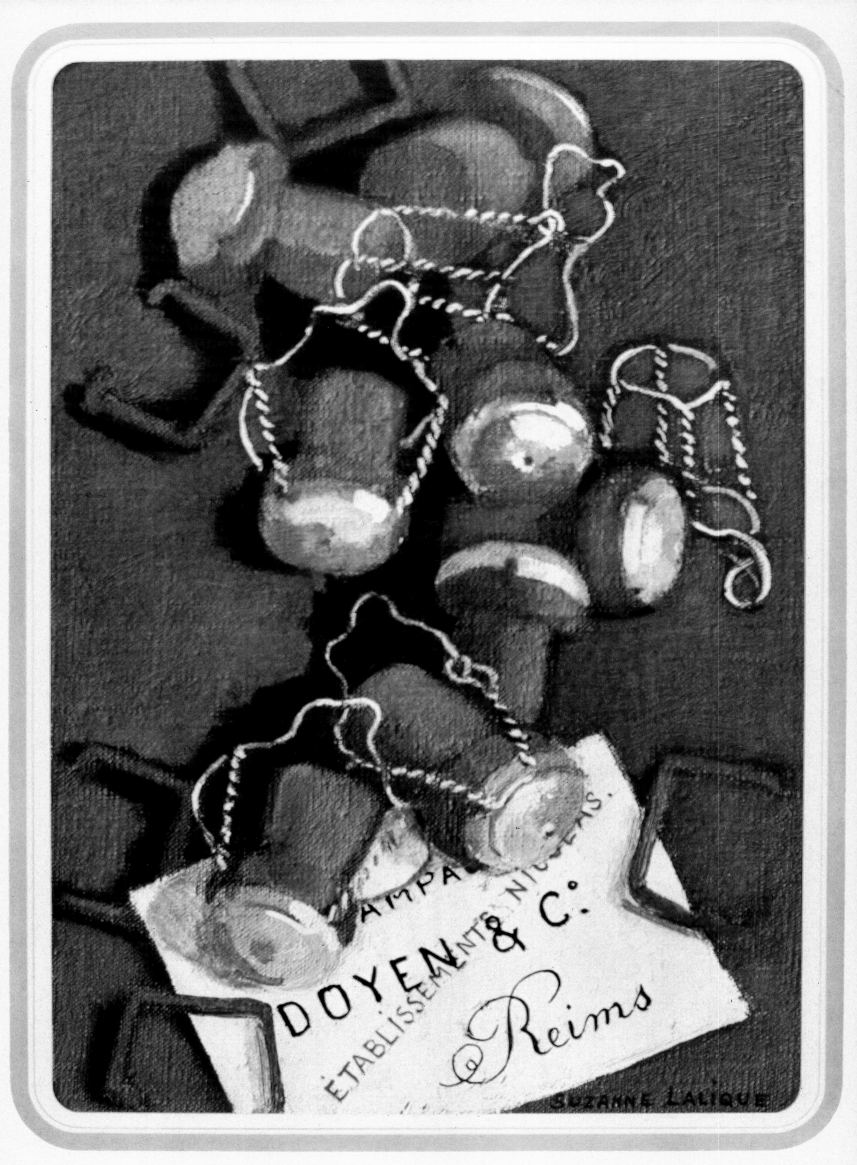

INTRODUCTION

If there is one truth universally acknowledged in viticulture, it is this: When you think about France, you think of wine, and when you think about wine, you think of France. This country, the most illustrious in the wine-producing world, owes its unequaled reputation to many factors, as much geographical as historical and human.

Anyone who travels across France cannot fail to be struck by the sheer variety of its landscapes, its soils, its local climates. From open pastures and meadows to gently sloping hillsides, from wide valleys to narrow gorges, high mountains, deep forests, endless moorlands, long roads lined with trees hundreds of years old, and garigue (the dry scrubland of southern France perfumed with wild herbs); from cliffs plunging into the sea to sandy beaches whose dunes stretch to infinity, from the Atlantic to the Mediterranean: France is a land of diverse terrain.

Underlying that diversity are the three climatic zones into which experts today divide the country: oceanic, continental and Mediterranean. We could likewise divide France into three parallel zones according to mentality and culture. The fresh Atlantic air somehow puts me in mind of windblown wines, those that travel the world. The Mediterranean heat calls to mind the image of sun-drenched wines, shared among friends. And finally, the continental climate suggests spiritual wines, those crafted by monks, sipped on Sundays at home with family.

The reality, however, is more complex. Across France, the transition from one climatic zone to another is gentle, even imperceptible. The result is an extraordinary mosaic of terroirs in which Nature seems to have taken pains to correct her own excesses. Thus in the hot, dry and often stormy southern Rhone Valley, the mistral, a wind that blows constantly from the north, has a drying effect on the air that protects agriculture, including the vineyards, from mildew and other diseases. Corsica's steep mountainous terrain creates a wide diurnal temperature shift at harvesttime that enables optimal maturation of the grapes' skins and seeds while preserving the fruit's freshness. The gentle climate of the Pays de la Loire allows the most varied agriculture in France. In Champagne, the winds from the North Sea, together with the region's chalky soils, constitute a natural climate regulator that protects the vines from frost and from the often heavy rains of winter and spring. The resulting multitude of microclimates yields France's wide array of appellations d'origine contrôlée, which have earned the country the nickname le jardin viticole, "the wine-growing garden."

Beyond France's rich urban and artistic heritage, the multiplicity of its landscape is one of the principal sources of the country's attraction to visitors from all over the world. As the planet's No. 1 tourist destination, France offers the same richness to wine lovers eager for new discoveries. For this magnificent "garden" is as varied in its geology as in its vegetation. Across the country, grapevines plunge their roots down into soils ranging from granitic to volcanic, from sand to limestone/chalk, clay, loam, gravel, silt and schist (among others), all more or less rich in minerals. Granitic soils produce wines firmly, tightly and squarely structured; red-clay soils yield fruity aromas and a rounder profile. Volcanic soils contribute iron or sanguine notes. Active calcareous soils—those with a high level of calcium carbonate or calcium oxide (lime)—give a wine a lively saline finish. Schist has a pronounced mineral signature. France's diverse climates combine with the country's assorted soils and the equally wide range of slope and aspect in its vineyards to create wine-growing landscapes of infinite variety, from Bordeaux's lovely chateaux to the micro-mosaic of Burgundy's vineyards, from the sloping coteaux of Champagne and Savoy to the Rhone's terraced estates and the steeply pitched plantations of the Jura Mountains. Add to all this the vast collection of varietals grown in France, and the result is an infinite array of wines, a multihued palette of incomparable richness.

Yet what would land and soil be without the men and women who have worked and cared for the vineyards? If France is the country where wine cultivation has achieved a quintessential refinement emulated worldwide, the credit, obviously, is theirs. Whether they were wise monks, shrewd merchants or winegrower-farmers who have passed down their knowledge from one generation to the next, all these men and women have woven a history envied worldwide. It was monks who first developed from scratch a classification system for the wine-growing estates of Burgundy, in an era when they were organizing the region's towns and countryside in ways still perceptible today. And it was indeed monks who originated the entire European viticultural tradition, particularly in the Mediterranean basin, where the Church was strongly present, and reaching all the way north to Champagne and the German wine-growing lands. Regarding the commercialization of wine, it is Bordeaux that made the most decisive contribution, with the famous classification of the estates on the Left Bank of the Garonne in 1855. This system was based directly on the market value of wines in the trade with British merchants, and therefore indirectly on the wines' quality, since the best wines of Bordeaux had already been for a century and a half the world's most highly prized—and high-priced. As for Champagne, the third of France's three universally famed wine-growing regions, it represents a synthesis of the Burgundian and the Bordelais approaches. To Burgundy, Champagne owes its monastic influence; to Bordeaux, the model of the great houses and famous brand names that have made Champagne renowned far beyond the borders of France.

It was also French winemakers who were the first to transfer their wines from barrels and casks to bottles with cork stoppers, which allowed them to be shipped and to improve with age. Across the centuries, France has also

enhanced wine's sublime magic by building upon viticultural tradition with innovative techniques, striving ceaselessly to unite savoir-faire, analysis and discovery, developing a form of cultivation that respects soil and vine, all the way up to the emergence of biodynamics. This culture of excellence reigns virtually everywhere in French winemaking. France's great wine traditions—the distinguished terroirs, the wines that can travel and age successfully for decades— are incarnate in the figure of the passionately devoted winegrower, the ultimate author of emotional experiences as essential to wine lovers as they are universal.

France has further played a key role in developing the sundry crafts and trades connected to winemaking, practiced by so many noble artisans who have contributed to building the production of wine into a national institution. Nowhere else are these professionals so highly respected for their skills, appreciated for their personalities, valued for their knowledge. In France, we cherish our relationships with all the gens de bouche—winegrowers and winemakers, sommeliers, maître d's, chefs—for the exchanges we enjoy with them contribute to memorable moments in our lives. We place so much trust in these great professionals of the culinary and viticultural arts and remain deeply indebted to them always.

Pierre-Auguste Renoir, *Luncheon of the Boating Party*, 1880-81, oil on canvas, 130.2 x 175.6 cm, The Phillips Collection, Washington, D.C.

ALSACE

Alsace is the most continental wine-producing region in France, and the farthest inland. The region is particularly dear to my heart, because it was there that I embarked on my career. The first wine I ever identified in a blind tasting, thirty years ago, was Alsatian; and Alsace was the first wine-growing region I ever visited, before taking even the first steps on my way to becoming a sommelier. That's why I cannot speak of this region except as a fervent advocate. Alsace is rich in great winemakers. For proof, consider how widely exported the region's wines are: especially to Italy and Asia, but globally, in fact, for Alsace's white wines are welcomed everywhere as warmly as those from any other part of France.

Five white grapes dominate here: Riesling, muscat, gewürztraminer, pinot gris and Sylvaner. Among reds, pinot noir is preeminent. The region counts fifty-one grands crus, each of which can be either dry or sweet. The latter include late-harvest wines, ice wines or those made via the sélection de grains nobles (noble rot) process. In almost all cases, the region produces single-varietal cuvées. The result is an exceptionally varied array of choices.

That's why I often say that you could draw up a wine list comprising solely Alsatians. Every palate would be satisfied and every plate perfectly matched. Alsatian Sylvaners are light, dry and a touch green, while the Rieslings are tenser and more mineral, with citrus notes. The pinot gris offer licorice and quince flavors with a bit more fleshiness and a rounder structure. The muscats are delectably aromatic and light; the gewurztraminers, exotically spicy and delicate. A dry Alsatian white is always a food-friendly treat. Think Riesling with langoustine carpaccio and caviar;

A tasting of Grand Cru Schlossberg is accompanied by local *Brezels. Following pages, from left:* The Vosges mountain
range in the haze, near the Schlucht pass and Hohneck summit; working in Alsace, early to mid-nineteenth century.

12

"We make the wine that we like and that we wish to defend. And if our clients like our wines, then so much the better. But it's also a question of freedom; the freedom to follow our instinct and to make wines that have a real story to tell."

— Céline Meyer, winegrower, Domaine Josmeyer

pinot gris with monkfish in a lemon-balm-scented jus; muscat with asparagus in mayonnaise sauce; Sylvaner with smoked trout; or gewurztraminer with Muenster cheese. Every one of these pairings is sheer joy for the taste buds. In their off-dry or sweet versions, nothing is better than an Alsatian Riesling with rhubarb pie; a pinot gris with a foie gras terrine; a muscat with apples in caramel sauce; or a gewurztraminer accompanying a South African baby Victoria pineapple with vanilla ice cream.

Alsace's vineyard soils are often granitic, yet schist, clay, limestone-chalk and volcanic terroirs are also found. With weather that can vary widely year to year, from hot to cool and dry to rainy, the Alsatian winegrower's craft is exacting. The region includes at least thirty high-quality estates that produce a wide variety of wines—tastings here can really take time. Alsace's greatest wines are all grand cru whites, often dry—though I have a preference for those gently caressed by just one or two grams of residual sugar, for their abundant charm and greater complexity. In recent years, thanks to a warming climate and the tireless efforts of certain winegrowers such as Jacky Barthelmé of Domaine Albert Mann, the local pinots noirs are excellent. All deserve a place of honor in your cellar.

As is equally true of some of France's other wine-producing regions, Alsace offers an immense variety that remains insufficiently known, and which deservedly appeals to curious wine lovers. A visit to Alsace should convince anyone that, beyond the three best-known wine regions of Bordeaux, Burgundy and Champagne, France offers a wealth of great and noble wines—and that in this regard, Alsace is not to be ignored.

The old town of Strasbourg, also called the "Petite France" ("little France"), has been listed as a World Heritage Site by UNESCO since 1988.

17

Whether in Strasbourg or Riquewihr, the Alsatian streets are full of charm, attracting visitors from around the world.
Following pages, from left: A summer tasting while overlooking the Alsatian vineyards; view of Hunawihr in the Haut-Rhin, along the wine route.

Mathieu Deiss and his father Jean-Michel, of Domaine Marcel Deiss. *Opposite:* At the Lucien Albrecht *domaine,* grapes are always harvested by hand to maintain quality. *Following pages, from left:* The oldest barrel of white wine at the Cave Historique des Hospices, a historic wine cellar in the heart of Strasbourg; tasting a Pinot Gris from Domaine Weinbach, one of the most important winegrowers in Alsace.

Liebe Freund, ich thue Euch hiermit Kund,
Hier liegt ein Wein um diese Stund'
Der wuchs, sag ich, gewiss und wahr
Als man zählet 1472 Jahr
Kam er in das Spital hinein,
Da der Burgunder Krieg ist gesein.

This page and opposite: Guests who stay at the charming Relais & Châteaux Le Chambard in Kaysersberg can enjoy a delicious typical Alsatian breakfast.

No matter the season, wine tasting can always be enjoyed throughout Alsace.

"Nowadays, we pick grapes that my grandparents could have only dreamed of harvesting, grapes that are well balanced and ripe."

— Albert Mann

"'Spiegel' is a German word meaning 'mirror'. It would appear to be named after its ability to capture the light of the rising sun and reflect it onto the vineyard throughout the day."

— Domaine Lucien Albrecht

The morning mist rises over the Alsatian village of Saint-Hippolyte, just south of Kintzheim, as seen from the Château du Haut-Kœnigsbourg, a twelfth-century hilltop fortress. *Opposite:* A bottle of wine from Domaine Agapé, a family-run winery started by Vincent Sipp in 2007.

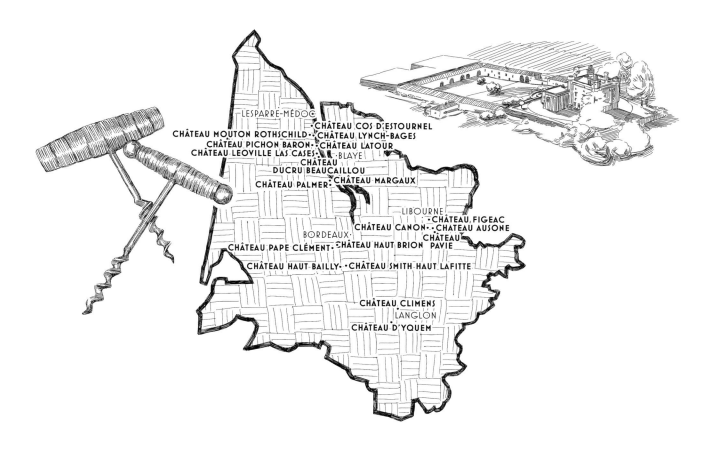

BORDEAUX

A great wine is one that can age. Yet age-worthiness in wine demands both a great terroir and winemakers who understand and know how to express its potential. If this is the true definition of greatness, then the wines of Bordeaux incarnate it to perfection.

In 1945, Mouton-Rothschild, under the Pauillac appellation, produced a vin du siècle, as did Cheval Blanc, in Saint-Émilion, for the 1947 vintage. These two terroirs are so extraordinary that all technical questions of winemaking there are strictly secondary; in fact, back in those years, the winemakers did not even consider them. At that moment, the world was just barely emerging from chaos. Six million European Jews had been savagely murdered, yet in Pauillac, humble winegrowers, including many women whose husbands had fought in the war or been imprisoned, created sublime wines—a triumph by the forces of life over the forces of death. These fin de guerre Bordeaux vintages bear witness to the winegrowers' ineradicable presence on their land and their resilience in the face of catastrophe. The wines' symbolism is all the more powerful given that the Rothschilds are one of the greatest, noblest Jewish families of Europe.

For some, the difference between Burgundy and Bordeaux is above all the difference between single-vineyard wines and those crafted by assemblage, between artisanal winegrower-winemakers and great estates, between micro-cuvées and large-scale production. Those who feel this way may also criticize Bordeaux on the grounds that it produces brand-name wines that lie in the hands of a few wealthy families and industrial conglomerates. Some have even reached the point of thinking that in Bordeaux there is no longer any terroir, only marketing.

"All that matters is that people like the wine. Here, we care about wine above all. Wine, wine, wine."

— Frédéric Engerer, Château Latour

"Traditionally here, the winery owner was also the farmer, the winemaker and the salesperson— someone involved with everything."

— Alain Vauthier, managing director, Château Ausone

Today, Bordeaux wine is made by more than 5,600 producers and châteaux, with sixty-five different appellations of Bordeaux wine.

"We manage the entire process, from the origin of the oak from the highest quality forests of France to the drying process of the mérains (stave wood), and the crafting of the barrel with a precise toasting degree."

— Florence Cathiard, Château Smith Haut Lafitte

In fact, in the 1990s the region was widely taken as a model for wine production outside France, prior to being more recently somewhat shunned. The price of the Bordeaux grands crus is the main cause of this phenomenon. The high prices commanded during the annual en primeur spring sales in 2005, 2009, 2010, and more recently in 2015 and 2016, repelled many among the Bordeaux faithful. In the long view, this is unfair. For in the field of wine, as in many others, we sometimes treat most harshly what we have most adored. Without doubt, in Bordeaux we rarely encounter a wine-growing sole proprietor, and the cellars lie beneath chateaux, not country homes or farmhouses or their outbuildings. Yet therein lies the region's identity—and its greatness. We cannot expect the proprietor of a chateau to go out and prune a vine any more than we would expect the owner of a Parisian mansion to cook or clean. We do well to remember that small is not necessarily better, and that Bordeaux offers an excellent price-to-quality ratio in many of its wines, including its crus bourgeois, the great chateaux' second wines, and wines from satellite appellations such as Canon-Fronsac, Lalande-de-Pomerol and Côtes-de-Bourg.

Because Bordelais vineyards are very ancient and, in many of the chateaux, production is substantial, wine lovers know that Bordeaux wines are exceptionally age-worthy. Among the best old vintages that I have drunk in my life, the great majority are Bordeaux or Sauternes, including a 1928 Margaux, a 1947 Cheval Blanc, an 1865 Latour, a 1945 Mouton or Lafite Rothschild (I cannot quite recall which), a 1929 Haut-Brion and an 1811 Yquem: all of these will remain in my memory forever. While a 15-year-old Latour will possess a certain structure, a 150-year-old Latour is something else again: a magnificent witness to a great history. In this region, some chateaux produce 200,000 bottles of exceptional quality annually—an incredible feat. In the face of such excellence on such a scale, let us not spoil our pleasure: in the wine world, Bordeaux remains unique.

I must add here that, if Bordeaux, among all the globe's wine-producing regions, has become a model that inspires winegrowers everywhere, it is simply because Bordeaux tops all the rest. In parts of Latin America, Australia, South Africa and California, winemakers swear by nothing but Bordeaux varietals: cabernet sauvignon, cabernet franc,

Opposite: British wine merchant Steven Spurrier was often described as a champion of French wine. *Following pages, from left:* At L'Intendant Grands Vins store in the heart of Bordeaux, fine vintages that date back to 1945 are displayed along the walls of an impressive circular stairway; a close look at the bottles in the cellar of Château Pichon Baron.

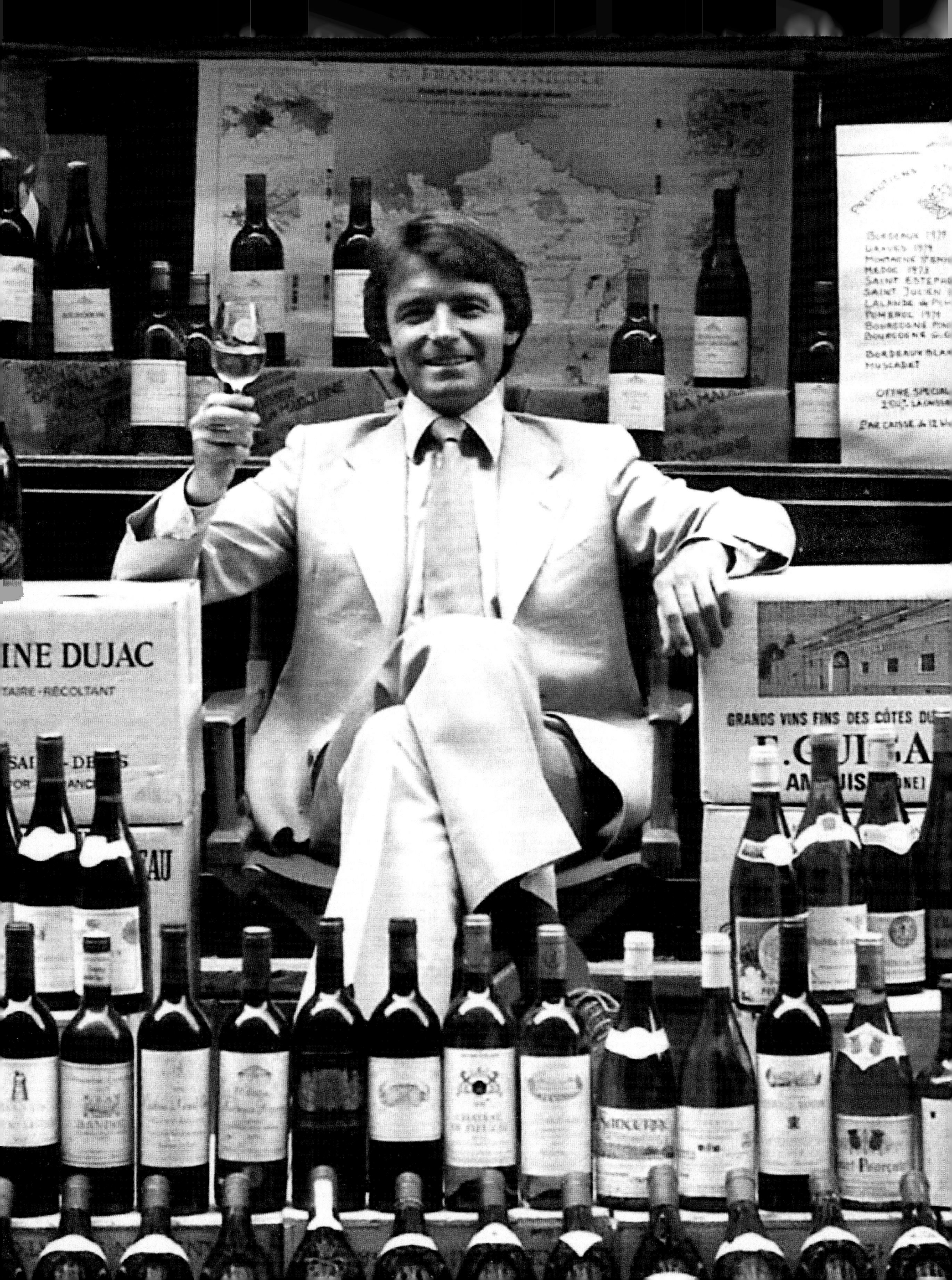
INE DUJAC
TAIRE-RECOLTANT
GRANDS VINS FINS DES CÔTES DU

"Time always reveals the truth. Our job is to move between temporalities."

— Thomas Duroux,
Château Palmer

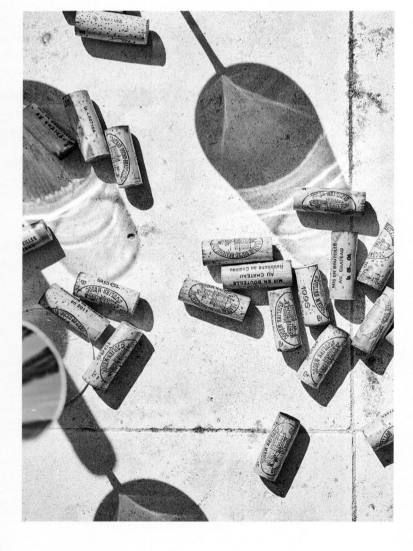

From bike tours around the region's key vineyards to harvesting with local producers to dinners and tastings full of flavors, the Bordeaux region offers an array of activities that delight every visitor.

"I spend my life making people happy with wine, and that's a kind of medicine."

— Pierre Lurton, Château d'Yquem

merlot. Even if, today, Burgundy's pinot noir is increasingly planted beyond the borders of its homeland, Bordeaux remains the symbol and the model of greatness, age-worthiness, quality and quantity of production.

On the Left Bank of the Garonne, the Médoc offers wine lovers a succession of prestigious chateaux, classified since 1855. The fidelity of Bordeaux's wine industry at its highest level to this classification system, now more than a century and a half old, is noteworthy—as is the persistent excellence and age-worthiness of the Médoc's wines.

On the Right Bank there reign two magisterial appellations: Saint-Émilion and Pomerol. Lying near the historic village of Saint-Émilion, the vineyards on the plateau surrounding Château Pavie, together with Château Ausone's steeply terraced holdings right nearby, are the Right Bank's greatest. (Of course it is well known that vineyards, like Ausone's, planted on France's sloping coteaux often produce good wine.) Saint-Émilion's classification system was instituted a century after the Médoc's (in 1955) and is updated every ten years (most recently in 2022)—a feature appreciated by wine lovers for its transparency. Pomerol enjoys the luxury of lying outside any classification system.

It is high time that we renew our respect for Bordeaux. Beyond doubt, the region boasts many exceptional terroirs. The intensely gravelly soils of Pessac-Léognan, the clay and limestone of Saint-Émilion, the fine gravels of Pauillac and the microclimate of Sauternes, strongly influenced by the Garonne, have inspired winemakers worldwide (even if Bordeaux's disciples may never equal her own masters…). The 1905 Lafite Rothschild that I was fortunate to taste the last time I visited that chateau was truly noble, simply outstanding. Great Bordeaux wines at their plateau of maturity can be in splendid form, just flawless, even a century after bottling. A great wine is able to age long, and if it is good young, it will achieve ideal ripeness in old age. In terms of delicacy, balance and longevity, Bordeaux has no equal. And indeed, wines that fall into the category of "Bordeaux blends" made anywhere else have never moved me the way the wines of Bordeaux itself do.

Visits to the four-hundred-year-old Château d'Yquem promise the discovery of an estate built around the notions of art and craftsmanship.

Above and opposite: Harvesting and tasting in the beautiful estates and vineyards of the Bordeaux region. *Below:* Stills from the French tragedy movie *You Will Be My Son*, directed by Gilles Legrand.

"Wine is the best thing God had invented to bring people together, like food." — Thibault Pontallier, Château Margaux

"Here, year after year, the hand of man has drawn up an exceptional vineyard, which we hold close to our heart."

— Bernard Magrez, Château Pape Clément

Following pages: In the heart of Saint-Émilion, Hôtel de Pavie offers panoramic views over the medieval village.

At Mouton Rothschild, the cellars comprise a bottle cellar, a reserve and the second-year cellar.
Opposite: Philippe Sereys de Rothschild at Mouton Rothschild.

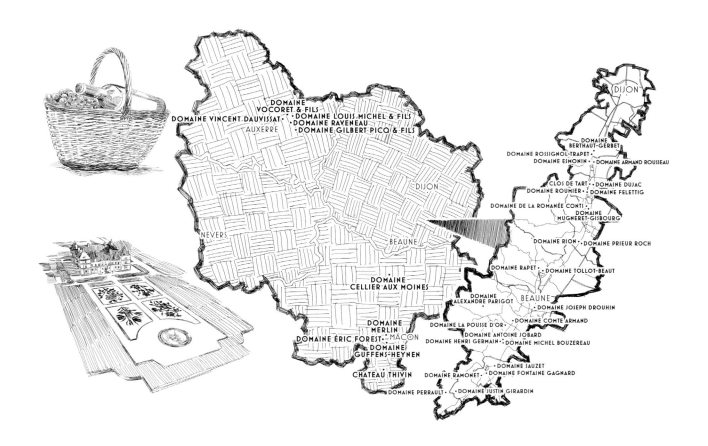

BURGUNDY

———◆———

Upon arriving in Burgundy, the visiting wine lover cannot help but be surprised. Can this really be the famous wine region whose excellence we have all heard so often proclaimed? Most of Burgundy's grands crus are represented by tiny vineyard parcels lying almost cheek by jowl. And instead of Bordeaux's spectacular chateaux, the visitor discovers a marvelous diversity of wine-estate architecture, in a veritable tapestry of vineyard landscapes, finely and densely woven.

A vineyard in Burgundy might surround a small church, rise toward a wooded area, open out, then be cut into small pieces, each bearing a different name. It might be classified according to the name of region, a local village or lieu-dit, or as a premier or grand cru. It is the division of wine-growing land into so many small units that results in the great number of Burgundian estates. I myself would count thousands of producers of great quality, including some that vinify as little as one barrique annually, perhaps three hundred bottles. Any estate that holds a monopoly over an entire parcel enjoys an extraordinary advantage, for quite the opposite situation often prevails. Such famed estates as La Tâche (a monopole of Domaine de la Romanée-Conti), Clos de Tart and a few others are exceptions that confirm the rule, for most of Burgundy's handkerchief-size vineyards are shared by several winegrowers, producing an equally varied array of wines, each expressing its own nuances. This particular topography goes back to the Cistercian monks who founded the first Burgundian vineyards, in the

For three centuries, Domaine Faiveley has been developed by seven generations of Burgundian winemakers. *Following pages, from left*: Exploring the vineyards of Côte de Nuits, a specific wine region in the heart of Burgundy; the Cluny Abbey is a former Benedictine monastery that was originally dedicated to saints Peter and Paul.

twelfth century. They developed the habit of naming each parcel they acquired, understanding that in order to express the identity of each, it was better to keep them separate rather than to amalgamate them.

In years with snowy winters, vineyards in which the snow melts the earliest have an advantage, as do those with pebbly soils that enable better drainage in rainy vintages, while in dry spells, it is rather those with clay soils that give the best results. All these geological and climatic factors together yield highly distinctive wines. Wine lovers can cultivate a passion for comparing, analyzing and choosing their favorites among the great diversity of the region's appellations and producers.

Burgundy presents us, above all, with paralleled complexity. In a swath of land only 60 kilometers (37.5 miles) wide stretching from Marsannay-la-Côte, at the northern end of the Côte de Nuits, to Maranges, at the northern end of the Côte de Beaune, the west side of the national highway is lined with a succession of villages whose premier and grand cru vineyards all lie mid-slope—for, according to a Burgundian proverb, "The best is in the heart" of the coteaux. Here we find the very essence of Burgundy: a subtle mosaic, bursting with colors, in which wines grown side by side could not be more different, like individuals from the same family, each with a unique character. The diversity of the region's wines is all the more remarkable given that Burgundy has for centuries been almost entirely devoted to just two varietals: pinot noir for reds and chardonnay for whites.

And yet, until the 1960s and '70s, Burgundy's wines had a hard time finding takers. Aubert de Villaine, co-owner of Domaine de la Romanée-Conti, has explained to me that, in the 1960s, he regularly made the trip to Paris in order to offer tastings of his wines to the city's leading chefs. In the same period, the winegrowers of the Meursault appellation would organize open-house days, when they would display their bottles on little tables so that people passing by could taste and buy their wines.

Things turned around decisively in the early 2000s, as the drinking public's taste changed drastically. The criteria for a great wine were no longer structure, concentration and viscosity (all typical of Bordeaux), but rather delicacy, lightness and indeed salinity. Prior to that time, a wine's élevage was the critical stage to which winemakers gave their keenest attention. Now, the situation is exactly opposite: terroir has become king once more, and the cépages are its mirrors. The wines of Burgundy, previously not terribly expensive, have come to represent the new taste—and the international wine market has done the rest. Prices have shot up to previously unimaginable heights, all the more so given that Burgundy's tiny production at the highest levels of quality never ceases to exert an upward pressure on prices.

The Route des Grands Crus in Burgundy offers, all by itself, a way to travel through the world of wine, even a sort of Via Sacra, a road of pilgrimage. Some follow the Camino de Santiago to Compostela on foot, others bicycle a leg of the Tour de France, but I advise you to travel the length and breadth of Burgundy, wandering its trails of delight, glass in hand. Here—while encountering the occasional tractor, cyclist and photo-obsessed tourist, of course—you will discover the very best that nature can do anywhere on earth with pinot noir and chardonnay.

The Moutonne is a small vineyard of just six acres, located on the Grand Cru hillside of Chablis.

60   *Following pages, from left:* Summer family days in the sunny Burgundy region; Philippe Pascal in his *domaine,* Cellier aux Moines.

The Burgundian landscape in October is a vision of the magnificent colors that follow the harvest, rich with a thousand tones of yellow, orange and chestnut. Traveling from North to South, we first encounter, on our right in the Côte de Nuits, Mazis-Chambertin, whose wines are austere and masculine, overlooked by Ruchottes-Chambertin to the west, with its delicate vintages. Next comes Chambertin–Clos de Bèze (densely textured); then Chambertin, the king of wine, noble but not overpowering; and the exquisite Latricières-Chambertin. On our left, opposite these magnificent terroirs, we may taste our way from the complexly woven wines of Chapelle-Chambertin to the delicate flavors of Griotte-Chambertin, which lead on to Charmes-Chambertin and Mazoyères-Chambertin, both seductively approachable.

Not two kilometers farther along, still in the Côte de Nuits, we find ourselves among the four musketeers of the Morey-Saint-Denis AOC. In the middle lie the domains of Clos de Tart and Clos des Lambrays, whose wines are rich and savory; to the north of the village of Morey-Saint-Denis itself are Clos de la Roche and Clos Saint-Denis, whose cuvées we may appreciate for their directness and elegance respectively. Moving south, Bonnes Mares, which sits astride the communes of Morey-Saint-Denis and Chambolle-Musigny, entices with wines of

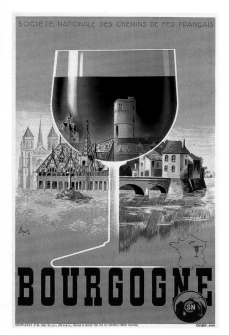

BOURGOGNE

"As maturity is approaching, grapes are tasted daily to choose the very best timing for harvest: a matter of perfect balance of sugar, tannins, and acidity."
— Cellier aux Moines

Harvesting, grading, and tasting local Burgundy wines, including at Domaine Lucien and Fanny Rocault in Saint-Romain (above).

bold structure, while the Chambolle-Musigny AOC itself offers some of Burgundy's most desirable vintages. At the foot of this sophisticated grand cru lies Clos de Vougeot; the part of its vineyard producing the most noble, refined juice faces the Combe d'Orveau premier cru and Musigny, while the part nearer the national highway produces more naturally rounded wines with a slightly bolder viscosity.

Once we arrive in Vosne-Romanée, we encounter the most precious gems among red Burgundies. This village is to wine what Rome is to history: an open-air museum. Romanée-Conti would be the Colosseum, the AOC's majestic and eternal symbol. Romanée-Saint-Vivant for me evokes the diverting Trevi Fountain, while Richebourg recalls the power of the Victor Emmanuel II Monument. La Romanée is the dignified Sistine Chapel, while La Tâche's wine has the scale of the Vatican. L'Échezeaux has the antique air of the Roman Forum; Grands-Échezeaux has the Pantheon's broad shoulders; and La Grande Rue suggests a stroll through the Campo de' Fiori. Such an analogy might seem incongruous, yet it nonetheless serves to remind us that wine grapes arrived in Burgundy from the Roman Empire, and that it was originally Benedictine and Cistercian monks who developed viticulture here to such a high level. Thus there exists an essential link between this region and the Rome of emperors and popes.

When we arrive on the Corton hill, in the Côte de Beaune, we discover the grandeur of its age-worthy reds and the magnificent whites of Corton-Charlemagne, spicy and mineral. These lead us to real treasures, the world's most highly sought white wines, grown around the Montrachet hill, which produces the ultimate of all chardonnays. Other neighboring grand crus include the distinguished Chevalier-Montrachet, higher up the hill; and below, Bâtard-Montrachet, with its rounded wine, which is in turn flanked by Bienvenues-Bâtard (very fine), to the north, and Criots-Bâtard-Montrachet (very lively), to the south.

Despite all these glories, Burgundian winegrowers have never compromised, never sold their souls for the sake of profit. They take care of business, but never, or hardly ever, allow it to keep them from their work in the vineyard. They promote their heritage, and what they cherish above all are conviviality and sharing; familial traditions; and asking the kind of questions that enable them to improve their wines. Upon arriving in the Côte-d'Or for the harvest in the summer of 2023, I was afraid of disturbing the work already underway, yet I was welcomed with open arms. The winegrowers were happy to receive me and to take me "backstage," to show me the grape-sorting tables and the steadily filling vats. I shared some exceptional midmorning snacks with their teams, washed down for the occasion with a magnum of their best wine. Beyond doubt, in Burgundy, the value of vineyard real estate will never trump human worth. The rarity of the region's wines is well established, yet it is still the winemaker's task to give them soul, to make them come alive. Despite their success, even the superstar winemakers remain unaffected, entirely human.

The Burgundian spirit is on full display during January's Saint-Vincent Tournante wine festival, organized by the Confrérie des Chevaliers du Tastevin (Fraternity of Knights of the Wine-Tasters' Cup) to celebrate the

"The story of the domaine is very closely linked with replanting old vineyards."

— Emmanuel Guillot, Domaine Guillot-Broux

Festivities and celebrations when harvesting in the Burgundy region.
Following pages, from left: Friends enjoy a wine tasting at Clos des Vignes du Maynes; La P'tite Cave,
the Parisian wine shop of Michel Thievin, a graduate of the Dijon oenology school.

"Burgundy was the winiest wine, the central, essential, and typical wine, the soul and greatest common measure of all the kindly wine of earth."

— Cellier aux Moines

Following pages, from left to right: Rooted in centuries of history and tradition, La Paulée, which started as a rural luncheon, is one of the most emblematic events on the international wine calendar; eating and drinking in good spirits with chef Ludovic Lefebvre.

"The plots are harvested very early in the morning. Having cooled during the night, the bunches are picked and immediately transported to the Cellier in small, ventilated crates, protected from the heat, to be pressed while they are still cold." — Cellier aux Moines

In the Burgundy region, vineyards are studded with majestic châteaux, providing visitors with a unique blend of cultural and gastronomic discoveries.

winegrowers' values of mutual aid. According to tradition, Saint Vincent, the patron saint of winemakers, assists them in coming to the aid of a neighbor in case of emergency by donating equipment, tools, or labor. I once had the pleasure of being the guest of honor and master of ceremonies for the Saint Vincent's Day festival when it was co-hosted by the neighboring villages of Morey-Saint-Denis and Chambolle-Musigny. There I experienced the marvelous atmosphere created by the local winemakers as they all throw open the doors of their vaults to offer wines collected over many vintages for tasting by the tens of thousands of wine lovers who annually make the pilgrimage to this happy occasion.

Other yearly events in a similar spirit include the Confrérie's Chapitre (literally, Chapter), a banquet held on the third Saturday in November at Clos de Vougeot. The invitation-only dinner highlights the warm welcome and magnanimity so typical of Burgundy, while subtly blending business with pleasure in a way that epitomizes the loyalty and trust binding winegrowers and their clients. The feast is followed on Sunday by the Hospices de Beaune charity wine auction and Le Roy Chambertin, a tasting held in conjunction with the auction; and on Monday by La Paulée de Meursault, a grand formal luncheon. The auction, known locally simply as "the wine sale," raises funds not only for the Hôpital de Beaune but for the region's poorest sick and elderly as well, among other causes. All these events together celebrate the end of the grape harvest; they also afford winegrowers a chance to invite clients and friends, and to uncork a few old bottles whose large format signifies the festival's generous spirit.

The generation of Aubert de Villaine, Lalou Bize-Leroy ("Queen of Burgundy"), Anne-Claude Leflaive, Henri Jayer, Henry-Frédéric Roch, Hubert de Montille, Dominique Lafon and Étienne Grivot (all now deceased or retired) won great success for their wines before passing the torch. Today, their amply qualified successors, such as Cécile Tremblay, Arnaud Mortet, the sisters Marie-Christine and Marie-Andrée Mugneret, Pascal Mugneret, Sébastien Caillat, the brothers Marc and Alex Bachelet, and Jean-Baptiste Bouzereau, among others, remain devoted to Burgundy. When they speak of the region, it is with a subtle insight, and a modesty too, that well expresses their intimate connection to the land. Each in their own way, these artisans perfectly incarnate their vineyards' and their wines' elegance, complexity, purity and even their spiritual qualities.

When you encounter any of the finest Burgundies, you cannot resist thinking, This is the greatest wine I've ever tasted! For here, all is finesse, a keen edge, understatement—nothing showy, but rather intimate, exquisite pleasures. As you continue your exploration beyond the Route des Grands Crus, you will discover the many great appellations of Chablis, the Mâconnais, the Côte Chalonnaise and Beaujolais, whose wines you may value for shared everyday enjoyment at the highest level. And there you will happily rediscover also a little bit of the Burgundy of bygone days—remarkable wines that offer not only great pleasure, but a very good value ratio too.

The beauty of the fall season at Chambertin Clos de Bèze. *Following pages:* A landmark in Burgundy, the Hospices de Beaune is a true architectural masterpiece and one of the most visited sites in the region.

Maynes, a domaine that has exclusively worked in organic farming since 1954. *Opposite:* Wine barrels in Burgundy cellars.

"We strive to contribute to the eminence of Burgundy by making wines that represent the diversity of our precious climates. We want to produce wines that blend strength with finesse and elegance."

— Erwan Faiveley, Domaine Faiveley

The Burgundy region makes up about three percent of French wine production. Each tasting provides visitors with a unique insight into the winemaking process.

CHAMPAGNE

———◆———

Everyone knows that when you lift a bottle of champagne out of the ice bucket, the party starts—whether for family, friends, or someone special. A glass of wine enjoyed alone always feels vaguely melancholy. Champagne is the opposite: popping that cork signifies celebration, meeting, sharing—and taking things up a notch. That's why, for centuries now, champagne has incarnated one of the most universal forms that happiness can take.

We can only admire the gently sloping hillsides, the immaculately aligned rows of vines—the whole geography of taste that has transformed this rather unforgiving land. Viticulture here is a real art, developed over hundreds of years, despite the severe constraints of an often cool and very rainy climate that makes achieving full maturity in wine grapes a challenge. The art of winemaking in Champagne relies, with rare exceptions, on blending wines made from multiple varietals, multiple vineyards and multiple vintages to achieve the remarkable results known worldwide. We have all drunk champagne, and we always will.

The history of champagne shades into legend, perhaps even myth. Is Dom Pierre Pérignon, a monk in the Benedictine Abbey of Saint-Pierre in Hautvillers, to be credited with the wine's invention? Or is it rather British importers in the late eighteenth century, who would add a bit of sugar (and some spices) to still wine from Champenois vineyards when they transferred it from barrel to bottle, restarting fermentation and developing the bubble-producing carbon dioxide? In fact, the invention of the méthode champenoise, the Champagne method,

At a local restaurant, the specials of the day can be paired with a bottle of Perrier-Jouët champagne. *Following pages:* Built in the eighteenth century and located next to Château Perrier, Perrier-Jouët's Maison Belle Époque houses the largest private collection of French Art Nouveau in Europe.

CAVES
RUINART PÈRE & FILS
REIMS
LES PLUS
PITTORESQUES
DE LA CHAMPAGNE
VISITE LIBRE

was something of a collective effort, for in addition to contributions of Dom Pérignon, we must note those of Dom Thierry Ruinart. While the legend will always retain a marvelous, even miraculous aura, the reality is doubtless more commonplace. Champagne is the result of a long evolution, including such developments as thick glass bottles; the metal agrafe (staple) to hold the cork in place; the definition of the region's terroirs; secondary fermentation; aging on the lees; disgorging; dosage, and so on. Countless winegrowers and winemakers have contributed over time to the champagne that we love today.

Whatever its mysterious origins, the method is complex, demanding time and care through several stages. First is the transformation of still wine into sparkling through a second fermentation in bottle triggered by the addition of sugar and yeast, which enables the wine to develop its famous tiny bubbles. In French, this phase is called the prise de mousse ("taking the foam"). Next comes long aging on the lees (spent yeast and sediment) that gives the wine its complex bouquet, silky structure and delicate effervescence. The length of bottle aging prior to release depends upon the kind of wine the winemaker wants to create. Regulations stipulate a minimum of fifteen months for simpler wines and three years for vintage champagnes. The most prestigious may age for many years, often up to ten or more, in order to obtain the richly varied bouquet, the elegant, refined palate, and the long finish for which great champagnes are famed, with their characteristic notes of gunflint and toast mingled with citrus zest and the "noble" mushrooms.

Viticulture in Champagne is possible thanks to two great assets: the chalky soils and the winds coming from the North Sea not far away. Together, soil and wind constitute effective climate regulators: the chalk allows the vine roots to dig deep rather than spreading out at the surface, limiting the risks of freezing in winter and summer drought, as the porous limestone acts like a sponge to retain moisture. Meanwhile, the maritime winds dry off the abundant spring rains. In this way, the vines are spared from extremes of weather.

Opposite, from left: Exploring the grounds of Ruinart, the oldest established Champagne house; a private cuvée of Krug Champagne.

"Champagne is also a wine; the aspect of the bubbles will become very fine and the wine aspect is becoming more obvious when you finish it all. I love the spices, the complexity and the intensity that we can reach in terms of flavors."

— Marie Charlemagne,
winemaker, Veuve Clicquot

One of the largest Champagne houses, Veuve Clicquot is rich with more than 250 years of wine heritage, which it constantly reinterprets. *Following pages, from left:* Stopping for a picnic in the Montagne de Reims Regional Nature Park, which spans sixty-five communes and is surrounded by the cities of Reims, Épernay, and Châlons-en-Champagne; in the dimly-lit cellars of Veuve Clicquot.

The nature of the soil is critical. Its limestone-chalk foundation dates back several million years, to the Mesozoic Era, when the region was covered by ocean. In some places, the pure, white chalk is visible right on the surface; elsewhere, it is mixed with sand or heavier soils (marl and clay). For centuries, limestone has been quarried throughout the region to construct homes, public buildings and monuments, and wine storehouses, leaving beneath them the famous crayères, long galleries, some deep underground, in which several million bottles age to perfection. A visit to some of Champagne's crayères is not only instructive but exciting, as places where winemaking technique is infused with the mysterious aura of stony labyrinths that seem to go on forever.

Champagne's winegrowers have succeeded in turning the terroir's challenging natural deficits to advantage. From a tricky winemaking process is born a wondrous elixir the whole world dreams about, not only symbolic of celebration and happy occasions but prestigious too: an exceptional wine for exceptional moments. For all that, Champagne has never compromised its standards. Nowhere else on earth have winemakers succeeded in making sparkling wines of such elegance, integrity, complexity and finesse: in a word, magic. Thanks to Champagne, a little bit of France is found on tables everywhere—and the region's wines help to drive sales of products from the country's other wine-growing areas as well.

"Craftsmanship comes with the strength of our team and the development of palate. Craftsmanship is the mix of technology and the human touch."
— Frédéric Panaïotis, cellar master, Ruinart

Harvesting days in the heart of the Champagne region.
Following pages: A mosaic depicting the unique winemaking process in the Champagne region.

RECOUPAGE

"Making wine is our life, making Champagne our reason for living. In fact, we are rather selfish. We like to make the Champagne we enjoy drinking: dry, pure, and full of the aromas found in our terroirs."
— Michel Drappier, Champagne Drappier

Both small-scale grower champagnes and those from the great houses can inspire. Among the latter, for example, to taste an S de Salon is to touch perfection; its texture, paired with a spoonful of caviar, is luxurious, highlighting the marriage of saline and mineral. And you can always count on a Krug Grande Cuvée as an aperitif with, say, foie gras on toast points. Meanwhile, today a multitude of grower-winemakers (récoltants manipulants) invite us to taste our way across their parcels to discover ultra-dry champagnes, with zero or next to no dosage, from young vintages as well as prestigious cuvées aged for half a century. I have had many such remarkable experiences. From Jacques Diebolt, the generous 1976, the magnificent 1953 and the eternal 1947 are engraved forever in my memory; Jacky himself opened all three for us to taste in his cellar—a moving moment. Eric Rodez, in Ambonnay, vinifies his pinot noir in small oak casks, without malolactic conversion, giving them a mouthfeel both rounded and profound. The great houses offer superb champagnes in this style, too, of course: at Bollinger, the 1952 R.D. is of peerless grandeur, while Vilmart's blanc de blancs, with its lanky silhouette, demands to be savored. And such producers as Georges Laval, Huré Frères, Jean Baptiste Geoffroy, Pascal Agrapart, Raphael Bérêche, Jacques Selosse, Mouzon-Leroux, Guiborat, Cédric Moussé and Fabrice Pouillon, among others, offer sparklers of great complexity, balance and personality to thrill us with the thousand nuances that only Champagne can offer.

Fresh, locally grown produce complements the region's best champagnes. Above, chef Pierre Gagnaire at Perrier-Jouët's Maison Belle Époque.

"Without human intervention, champagne will ruin itself."
— Pascal Agrapart, fourth-generation vigneron

Champagne presents an astounding range of savoir-faire. Starting not far from Paris and extending eastward as far as Troyes, the region counts seventeen grand crus plus a plethora of premiers crus, and typically ships more than three hundred million bottles annually. About half of this impressive figure is produced by the great houses, and tends to be highly upmarket. Yet many of the approximately two thousand small producers are well worth discovering too. I myself can count no fewer than two hundred remarkable artisans among them, and they continue to surprise me with the sheer multiplicity of expressions they create from their various holdings.

I am not afraid to say that Champagne combines the best qualities of Burgundy and Bordeaux, offering wine lovers prestigious houses that recall the great Bordelais chateaux together with the diversity and the high degree of technical sophistication of the numerous small winegrowers who produce, as in Burgundy, a few thousand bottles from each of perhaps five or six cuvées. Their assemblages are highly diverse: blancs de blancs and blancs de noirs, vintage and nonvintage, and ranging from zero dosage through extra brut to sweeter wines as well.

Champagne is without question securely installed in the global pantheon of wine—and not stepping down anytime soon. My advice to the curious wine lover in the know? Don't be afraid to climb up, too—all the way to the top.

Champagne houses are known to be run by members of one family, passing down knowledge from generation to generation.

"A champagne is ready when we are in symbiosis with the effervescence, the olfactory and gustatory aromas, and the texture in the mouth."

— Séverine Frerson, cellar master, Perrier-Jouët

Celebrating some of life's key moments with champagne dates back to fifth-century France and King Clovis, whose kingdom lifted glasses filled with local wine (from the Champagne region) in honor of his First Communion as King. *Following pages:* The cellars of Champagne Boizel, a sixth-generation Champagne house that has been in production since 1834.

"Every year since the foundation of the House, a new
Edition of Krug Grande Cuvée is created;
every year the inspiration will be the same,
but the creation will be totally unique and different."

— Olivier Krug, director of the House of Krug,
sixth generation of the Krug family

Founded by Joseph Krug in 1843, Krug Champagne mainly produces Krug Grande Cuvée
and is known for its toasted notes born from at least six years of aging *sur lie.*
Following pages, from left: Harvesting at the Veuve Clicquot wineries; the staff moves some
of the barrels in the courtyard of Champagne Bollinger.

A sunny afternoon exploring the vineyards of Champagne Richardot by bike.
Opposite: In Chavot-Courcourt, church and vines touched by sunset.

"I drink it when I'm happy and when I'm sad. Sometimes I drink it when I'm alone. When I have company, I consider it obligatory. I trifle with it if I'm not hungry and I drink it when I am. Otherwise I never touch it, unless I'm thirsty."

— Madame Elisabeth Bollinger, in the London Daily Mail, October 17, 1961

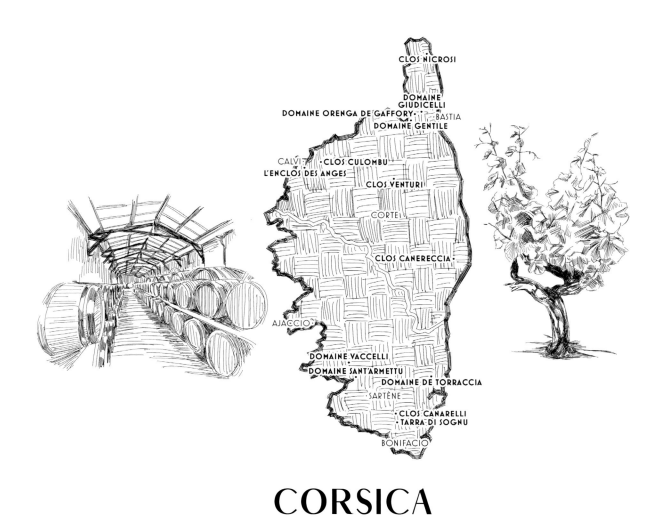

CORSICA

Corsica is like a mountain range in the middle of the sea—some of the island's peaks exceed 2,000 meters (6,500 feet). The coastline is ringed with landscapes each more beautiful than the last, and the interior is covered in dense forests or breezy maquis scrubland. No visitor can remain indifferent before the power and majesty of this magnificent chunk of rock in the Mediterranean—hence its nickname, the Isle of Beauty.

In wine-growing terms, I would sum up this natural paradise in a single sentence: Corsica offers new-world advantages in the heart of the Old. Meaning that the island's traditions remain faithful to the those of its European hinterland, but amid landscapes atypical of Europe—terroirs that remind me more of South Africa or Australia. Here the wine lover will discover scattered plantations closely entwined with the natural environment, a climate mingling extreme heat with cooling influences, respect for the oldest ancestral practices and their constant renewal in the vineyard. Native varietals dominate, which forward-thinking Corsican winemakers seek to align with contemporary tastes. The island's diurnal temperature shift enables the grape skins to ripen to perfection during the final weeks before harvest, yielding highly aromatic wines.

Corsica's wine-growing estates are almost all located close to the coast and tend to be somewhat isolated. After a long drive to reach Domaine Sant Armettu, one of the best in western Corsica, for example, I found the vineyard surrounded by a ravishing landscape of maquis, olive and fruit groves, and sheep pasture. The vines can

Breathtaking views of the sea and surrounding grounds from Clos d'Alzeto.
Following pages: The limestone cliffs of Bonifacio are home to the citadel and old town.

Following pages, from left: From the U Capu Biancu hotel, guests can access the nearby secluded beaches; the cliffs of Bonifacio look out over the Mediterranean.

From lunch to dinner, Corsica offers delicious fresh seafood that can be savored accompanied with local wine. *Following pages:* In the south, Domaine de Murtoli meets the waters of a cove.

"Space, nature, peacefulness, authenticity, welcome, lifestyle, and gourmet cuisine. There is something for everyone."

—Paul Canarelli, owner and founder of the Murtoli Estate

only benefit from such balanced polyculture—including the natural fertilizer provided by sheep and goats—which protects them from many vineyard diseases. Most Corsican estates are still single-family domaines, and the island as a whole boasts some thirty very important names. While these tend to be strongly concentrated toward the North, some are also found near Ajaccio, the capital, including Domaine Vaccelli, Domaine u Stiliccionu, not to mention Domaine Comte Abbatucci, a pioneer in adopting biodynamics.

Corsica's soils are varied. The entire southern end of the island is granitic, while the terroir surrounding the town of Bonifacio boasts impressive white limestone cliffs. Here, Yves Canarelli and his son at Tarra di Sognu create luminous wines, as does the nearby Domaine Zuria. In the North we find clay soils in the Patrimonio subregion, ideal for the native nielluccio varietal. Many other Corsican winegrowers enjoy an indisputably high reputation, including Yves Leccia, Muriel Giudicelli, Antoine-Marie Arena and Christophe Ferrandis at Clos Signadore. In the mountainous terrain near Corte, on the west coast, there is also schist. Here Manu Venturi, of Clos Venturi, sets the gold standard; I adore his Altare, a refined expression of the indigenous sciaccarellu grape. In the area around Calvi, farther north, the varietal rolle blanc, here called malvoisie, presents a strong profile: salinity, directness, brightness and length—and age-worthiness, up to thirty years. For all these reasons, Corsican malvoisie fully deserves the nickname Riesling of the Mediterranean. Notable Calvi domaines include Clos Culombu, Clos Landry and Enclos des Anges. And what can I say about the Cap Corse, one of the most beautiful wine-growing areas on earth? Here, in vineyards that seem to slope straight down into the sea, the particular varietal of the muscat grape yields very unusual and seductive dessert wines whose tropical-fruit notes are laced with a salinity due to the maritime influence, and which have a structure of great intensity and length. The muscats of Clos Nicrosi, Domaine Pieretti and Domaine Orenga de Gaffory deserve to be tasted at least once in a lifetime.

Corsica presents a very diverse array of wines, not remotely monolithic. The great majority of Corsican reds are good, grown with care by outstanding winemakers: floral, delectable, subtle. The whites, too, richly deserve notice. The alchemy of mountain, maquis and sea counts for a great deal. On the whole, Corsica's wines are endowed with intense aromas and open flavor profiles with charming accents. On the nose, they evoke ocean breezes, with marine nuances that enhance a deep and luminous robe. Typical notes include wild herbs, myrtle, oregano, basil and mint, with echoes of citrus and spice. In the mouth, the wines are suave and caressing, and laced with puckering tannins on the finish. For me, Corsican wines are always noble, yet with a deeply human touch—like the perfume that lingers in the scarf worn by a beloved woman, or her sweetly speaking smile. They are wines that marry marvelously well with the warm atmosphere that defines the Mediterranean way of life.

My advice: discover—or rediscover—Corsica and its wines. Accept an invitation to the slow rhythm of island life. Match the wines to authentic local products—from the pasture, the dairy, the garden. Here, nature reigns in majesty, and you can be sure of traveling the length and breadth of the isle in peace, for Corsicans remain determined to protect their environment from the noisy dangers of heedless industrial modernization.

At a store in Ajaccio devoted to Napoleon, this poster advertises the wines of Clos d'Alzeto.

VIN
CLOS D'ALZETO

ICI  HERE

Casa Buonaparte
Ajaccio

PARIS - LYON - MÉDITERRANÉE

LES CALANCHE DE PIANA

SERVICES AUTOMOBILES D'EXCURSIONS AUTOUR D'AJACCIO

For generations, Corsica has produced some of the finest French wines. Fifty-five percent of Corsican wines are rosé and most of the production takes place exclusively on the island. *Following pages, from left:* Sipping wine on the go at Clos Culombu; the table is set for lunch at Domaine de Murtoli.

"The advantage of an island is that we have a lot of diversity. That's the advantage of Corsica — the diversity we can have. That's what makes us rich and different from other great terroirs." — Sarah Giacometti, winegrower, Domaine Giacometti

"We had a Corsican wine that had great authority and a low price. It was a very Corsican wine and you could dilute it by half with water and still receive its message."
— Ernest Hemingway, A Moveable Feast

Whether from grapes grown by the sea or inland, the wines produced under Corsica's AOP appellations are steadily increasing in quality and quantity.

"In Corsica there is a unique ecological and panoramic reality: all the estates are on land surrounded by scrubland, mountains, or the sea... The landscapes are marvelous."
— Enrico Bernardo

Christian Imbert was an emblematic figure of Corsican wine-growing. The founder of Domaine de Torraccia, he was particularly known for his fight to defend indigenous grape varieties. *Opposite:* Overlooking the Corsican landscapes: The small island is home to more than thirty grape varieties and nine AOC regions. *Following pages, from left:* Celebrating summer at Clos Culombu, located near the communes of Lumio and Montegrosso; hosting at Tarra di Sognu.

"Corsica is very complicated. It is French, but it is not. First, we are Corsican, then we are French. When you're an island, you think differently than the continent."

— Yves Canarelli of Clos Canarelli

Locally grown produce, fresh cheese, and homemade meals accompany Corsican wines to perfection during celebrations and gatherings. *Following pages, from left:* For more than thirty years, Fromagerie Donsimoni has made fresh cheeses using only Corsican milk from their own herds; in the heart of Corsica, bed and breakfast A Chjusellina is set on a working farm, providing guests with a unique experience close to nature.

On the bay of Calvi between Lumio and Montegrosso, Clos Culombu looks over the land but is only a few minutes away from the sea. *Opposite:* Grapes are better harvested on a cool, dry day, so they can be stored longer. *Following pages:* A dinner setup at Domaine de Murtoli. Guests can taste the products of the working farm such as the veal and the lamb, as well as the fruits and vegetables from the kitchen garden.

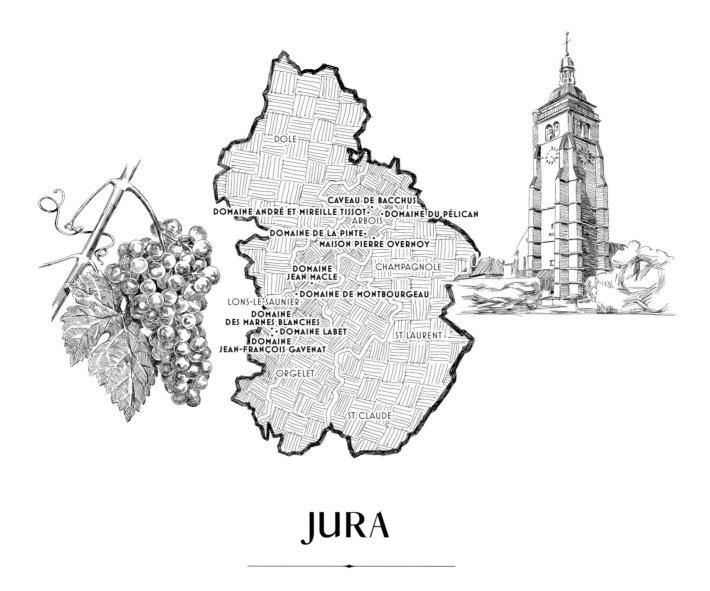

JURA

I have a real passion for the Jura, the greenest of all of France's viticultural regions. I love the Jura first because there you find so many people determined to protect its forests and rivers, indeed the whole natural environment, and who do not much appreciate the capitalistic turn that wine-growing has taken in other places. Second, because the Jura is the cradle of the French oxidative style and of natural wine. To be sure, we might harbor some reservations regarding certain excesses of the latter approach—I'll return to this topic below—but still, in the Jura, authenticity truly counts. And finally, because the region's wines can really jolt us out of our rut: to the extent that they resemble no others, they stimulate curiosity and demand attention. The Jura's winemaking is provocative—it raises genuine questions. Jurassien winegrowers pose a challenge through their uncompromising determination to remain who they are, against all odds. This explains why, for decades, many wine drinkers did not appreciate their products. For a sommelier, as recently as twenty years ago, selling a bottle of Château-Chalon was an achievement—its walnut and oxidized-apple flavors were simply a turnoff to many wine lovers.

Yet we should face facts: vin jaune—the "yellow wine" that is the Jura's most characteristic product—constitutes a real feat of winemaking. Recall that this nectar must age for at least six years and three months in barrel, while a voile (veil), a film of active yeast, grows on its surface. The wine that evaporates is not topped

up, so the voile allows the wine beneath to oxidize only partially, preventing it from turning sour. This miraculous process is shared with only one other great wine: sherry. How does such a method of élevage not go catastrophically wrong? The magic lies in the fact that the voile yeast only grows within a certain range of alcohol content and acidity and is then sustained by the presence of alcohol and oxygen, protecting the wine. Without this miracle, the wine would turn to undrinkable vinegar. One critical step is the breaking of the chapeau (cap) of yeast. The winemaker then proceeds to rack the wine into specially shaped bottles that hold just sixty-two centiliters (twenty-one ounces), equaling the percentage of each liter of the original new wine that is left after six years of evaporation. Many factors contribute to this alchemy: first, there is the cépage, savagnin; then the local climate, which is cool and damp; the natural presence of the yeast in the cellars; and finally, of course, the winemaker's constant vigilance.

The result is unique—and simply extraordinary. Vin jaune is surprising, with delicate but distinct flavors of almond and hazelnut over a very saline bass note. For food pairings, the choice is wide: think smoked fish, poularde aux morilles (fattened chicken with morels) or chicken à la comtoise (in a sauce of white wine, crème fraiche and Comté cheese), among other dishes. But if you want to persuade a reluctant drinker, offer a glass of vin jaune with a chunk of three-year-old Comté: no one can fail to be won over by such a perfectly balanced harmony. By comparison, any other white wine will seem bland. Your friend will soon become a vin jaune devotee. And who knows? You both might also fall for the Jura's rare vin de paille, a strong sweet wine made with dried grapes, also richly flavorful, and extraordinary accompanying a chestnut cake or a salted-caramel praline.

The Jura's red wines are made chiefly from trousseau and poulsard. They tend to be very pale in color, fruity or floral in character, and to offer just a touch of acidity. These are light, subtle and elegant wines, which prevailing tastes in the last few years have increasingly appreciated, and which can age marvelously. I have experienced this myself with wines made in the 1980s by Jacques Puffeney, a happy discovery: sapid, refined, with great complexity and length, these vintages were practically sufficient all by themselves. Meanwhile, certain Jura dry whites, made from savagnin and chardonnay, are equally worth discovering and can be drunk with relish throughout an entire meal. I love them for their flavors of fresh stone fruits, dried fruits, gunflint, tisanes and mountain wildflowers. They possess a lovely harmony and a wide array of nuances, despite all stemming from a single appellation, the Côte de Jura.

Natural wine was made in the Jura long before the advent of the global natural-wine movement, and the region can boast a great number of estates that lead the way in this area. The high quality of their production speaks for itself among true aficionados. Their common denominator is a kind of purism, a quest for the absolute. In the village of Pupillin, Pierre Overnoy, who founded his eponymous estate in 1968, launched the movements for both natural (organic) and biodynamic winemaking. His exceptional enterprise has been maintained with

Between Burgundy and the Swiss border, the Jura region is dotted with vineyards, waterfalls, caves, and valleys with high cliffs.
Following pages, from left: Though it is a small wine region, the Jura is responsible for some of France's most characteristic wines;
Jacques Puffeney pours some wine for a tasting in his barrel room in Montigny-lès-Arsures.

brio by his collaborator and successor, Emmanuel Houillon. Others have followed Overnoy's lead. Their gospel is a rejection not only of chemicals in the vineyard but also of industrial agribusiness as a whole, which they oppose with the determination to remain faithful to their principles, to pursue their logic to its limits. Thus the Jura was also among the first wine-growing regions to eliminate or considerably reduce the use of sulfur in its wines, a move that has broadened the perspective of many winemakers worldwide, with positive results. The renunciation of sulfur demands an élevage of impeccable quality, otherwise the wine will reveal multiple flaws, such as vinegar, barnyard or cured-meat notes. But when it all comes together, the results are just fantastic.

As I have suggested, natural wines can be the best—or the worst. When a natural approach in the cuverie has not been preceded by work on the vineyard soils, with respect for the natural vegetation— without a perfect symbiosis between the human and the environment— "natural wine" amounts to little more than trendiness. In fact, natural wine is ancient: it is the wine in a carafe on a winegrower's own table— wine made by an artisan only for personal use and not for sale, by one who believes that shipping wine, even the shortest distance, can only harm it. Yet the Jura has succeeded in distancing itself from this austere image by cultivating a reputation for a meticulously noninterventionist approach that yields wines with bold personalities. Doubtless there is a risk that some of the region's exports may be compromised by shipping and the vagaries of storage, but the Jura remains nonetheless unique.

For me, an affection for Jura wines constitutes an excellent sign of good taste, open-mindedness and curiosity in a wine lover. Such a person is willing to taste their way toward the unknown—a tough challenge. But what is a true wine lover if not someone willing to be shaken out of their habits as they discover new, unique, surprising tastes? For so many reasons, I can only invite you to join me on a gustatory adventure in the Jura. I guarantee that you will head home charmed, even enchanted.

At the heart of the village of Bois-d'Amont, the Musée de la Boissellerie is housed in a restored sawmill. Visitors can admire the tools, machines and know-how of artisan woodworkers. *Following pages, from left:* Chef Jean-Paul Jeunet and second de cuisine Yoann Constanty gather fresh herbs in the countryside above Arbois; cheese and wine pairing for a tasting at Le Grand Jardin restaurant, in Baume-les-Messieurs.

"There is an infatuation with the Jura
that wasn't there before and a great
energy amongst the organic producers."
— Alice Bouvot, winegrower, Domaine de l'Octavin

In 1985, Jean Berthet-Bondet took over a local vineyard that had not been producing wine for more than fifty years and turned it into one of the key wine producers of the area. *Opposite:* In the spring and summer months, the façades of Château-Chalon come to life, sporting vibrant flowers.

Local products—especially wine—can be enjoyed year-round at Château de Germigney (*top left and bottom right*), a former eighteenth-century hunting lodge set in a lush park. *Following pages:* The natural waterfall of Baume-les-Messieurs is full of protruding rocks; down in the valley, a village full of charm awaits.

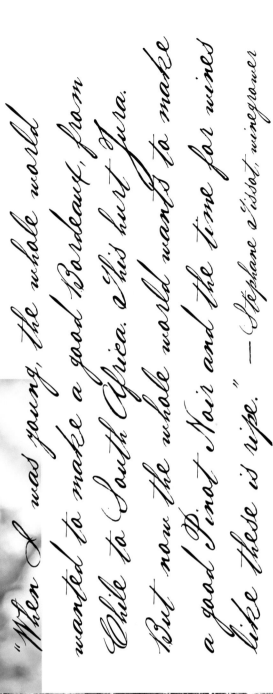

"When I was young, the whole world wanted to make a good Bordeaux, from Chile to South Africa. This hurt Jura. But now the whole world wants to make a good Pinot Noir and the time for wines like these is ripe." — Stéphane Tissot, winegrower

In the Jura region, the domaines and castles welcome guests for exclusive tastings on the grounds of their estate. *Following pages:* Encountering local celebrations while exploring the Jura wine road.

"An affection for Jura wines constitutes an excellent sign of good taste, open-mindedness, and curiosity in a wine lover."

— Enrico Bernardo

"In the past decade, much has evolved in the Jura wine region: new generations have taken over at traditional wine producers; there is an impressive number of brand-new vignerons; and there are other exciting producers that have emerged." — Wink Lorch, author of Jura Wines

The soft Vacherin Mont-d'Or cheese is a specialty of Vaud, across the Swiss border. *Opposite:* The shadow of a bottle and glass of wine reflect on an oak barrel of 2018 Savagnin yellow wine. *Following pages, from left:* Church steeples rise above the villages of the Jura; a Roman Catholic chapel in Ronchamp, Notre-Dame du Haut is one of the seventeen buildings imagined by Le Corbusier that have been added to the UNESCO World Heritage List.

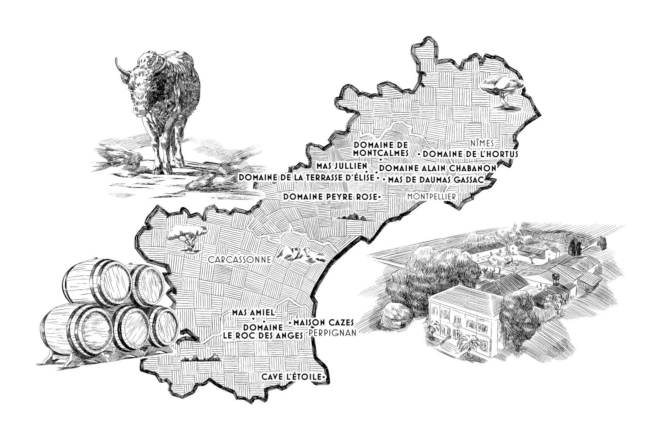

LANGUEDOC-ROUSSILLON

This sprawling wine-growing region is divided into two parts: in the West, bordering the Spanish province of Catalonia, is Roussillon, whose principal city is Perpignan; in the East, surrounding the cities of Narbonne, Béziers, Montpellier, and Nîmes, is Languedoc. The first thing to know is that Languedoc-Roussillon offers many little-known treasures—and at very reasonable prices.

Roussillon is home to the Collioure AOC, where vines are grown on impressive terraces in gray schist soils that produce great gastronomic wines. Among white grapes, grenache blanc dominates; among reds, grenache rouge. These wines are somewhat underappreciated, perhaps simply because they come from the southernmost part of France, so far from Paris—they await their turn in the spotlight. Still, a wine lover who sips a Collioure blanc, with its pretty salinity, accompanying fresh anchovies flash-marinated in olive oil, will have a fine time—it's a pairing as delectable as the well-known duo of champagne and caviar. Mediterranean sun, a hot climate, sea winds, scarce rainfall, vineyards surrounded by sun-baked wild herbs: all these factors give Collioure's wines a light, sapid touch and a remarkable richness of flavors. That's why, in my view, so many of Roussillon's wines truly are hidden nuggets.

Following pages: An aerial view of Bram, a charming city constructed in a circular layout around a central church.

"One of the great lessons of recent years is that a new generation of winegrowers (...) has demonstrated that it is possible to produce great wines in Languedoc-Roussillon, freeing themselves from the influence of Bordeaux, Burgundy, and Côtes du Rhône wines, and thus define their own wine identity." — Jérôme Joseph, winegrower, Calmel & Joseph

Other Roussillonnais gems are the sweet fortified vins mutés of Rivesaltes, Maury and Banyuls. Like sweet wines in general today, these suffer from not being in fashion, though that in no way prevents them from retaining their legendary status: these wines age so well that they can last a century. Their fans will match them with blue cheeses, or chocolate—and they work with sweet or bitter. All these high-quality wines are sensational at the end of a meal, but I like to think of them as "wines for meditation." A glass of fifty-year-old Rivesaltes or Banyuls between meals, paired with something sweet, perhaps marzipan, is delicious. I well remember a Rivesaltes Cuvée Aimé Cazes 1963 of rare beauty, at once intense, persistent and complex, with a lovely, brilliant, deep amber hue, and offering notes of figs, Zante currants and other dried fruits, honey and spices. This was a wine that led me far from the beaten path to explore new ones. The wines of Banyuls are spicier, slightly smoky, with prune and jammy flavors: sensuous, rare, precious, delicate, full of distinction. To sum up, the wines of Roussillon, for those who know how to enjoy them, offer understated luxury—sheer excellence.

While Roussillon remains somewhat undervalued, Languedoc over the last half century has gone from strength to strength. Vast and highly productive, Languedoc has succeeded in making high-quality wines that have been valued all the more by wine lovers for their reliably low prices, especially in the early 2000s. More recently, with the shift in fashion away from powerful, highly structured wines in favor of those with more refined and subtle flavors, Languedoc was the first to suffer. Once again, the region had to reinvent itself. Today, the region's viticultural industry has come down on the side of organic, biodynamic and natural winemaking, for all of which local conditions are favorable.

Now, winegrowers throughout Languedoc-Roussillon find themselves facing a new challenge: the warming climate, which hit here earliest among all French wine regions. When the temperature reaches 35 to 40° C (95–104° F) for three weeks in July, the canopy shrivels and there is still a month left before harvest, the winegrower's work becomes very complicated indeed. While the challenge is real, the region's means for adapting to it are no less substantial. Languedoc-Roussillon is bursting at the seams with skilled winegrowers, and many of its vineyards are planted with old vines, which are naturally more resilient in the face of extreme weather. Such estates as Mas Jullien, Domaine de Montcalmès, Domaine Peyre Rose and Domaine La Terrasse d'Élise feature fine indigenous varietals. Well served by their adherence to ancestral traditions, they have led their appellations to increased recognition, offering approachable, well-balanced wines produced with care. These days, the winegrowers tend to harvest their fruit a bit earlier than in the past, and they are emphasizing their higher-altitude vineyards. They minimize pruning in canopy management, and take a light-handed approach to vinification, with limited extraction during the fermentation phase, in order to obtain wines with balanced structure. The result is wines to share with friends on the spur of the moment, a pleasure to drink with the olive-oil-based cuisine of the South of France. Think Mediterranean fish with the salty whites, country lamb with fresh herbs with the luscious reds or summer vegetables with the region's fruit-forward rosés.

Coffee and wine sipped in the local cafés of the Languedoc region. *Following pages, from left:* Not far from Montpellier, Domaine de Biar welcomes guests and visitors between sea and city. Here, the horses at the estate at sunset; Calmel & Joseph wines are produced at the heart of two hundred hectares of vineyards.

In Languedoc-Roussillon, families of winegrowers welcome guests to explore the grounds of their estates and taste locally made wines. *Following pages, from left:* In the vineyards of Château L'Hospitalet, which was voted one of the top ten best French châteaux for weddings; a building dating back to the fourteenth century, the Château Bas D'Aumelas has been in the Albenas family for more than two hundred years. Here, fresh snacks with wine in the garden.

"Today, we are seeing the vibrancy of our terroir. There is great potential to age these wines. At the end of the day, you need to learn and understand your terroir."

— Gérard Bertrand, winegrower, Château l'Hospitalet

A UNESCO World Heritage Site, the Arles Roman amphitheater could accommodate up to 21,000 spectators back in 80-90 AD. *Opposite:* Cypress trees can be found throughout the Languedoc region; they are a symbol of eternal life and stay green year-round. *Following pages:* Laurent Calmel and Jérôme Joseph started Domaine Calmel et Joseph in 1995, creating a diverse estate made up of vineyards, beehives, and lavender fields.

"Each region is different. Languedoc AOP has the size of Burgundy and has an ambition of excellence, so that some of the greatest wines of Languedoc have that same ambition and are now reaching the top levels."

— Miren de Lorgeril, winegrower, Maison Lorgeril

The lush beauty of Languedoc vineyards. The region's AOC wines are mostly red blends made with Syrah, Grenach, Carignan and Mourvedre. *Following pages, from left:* At the medieval Château des Guilhem, the interior of the cellar has been designed for optimal conservation and winemaking; the wheat fields of the Languedoc region take on a golden color when basking in the sunshine.

The art of horse riding and the Romani culture have been part of Languedoc history for centuries. *Previous pages:* A capture from Tony Bonanno's fine-art photography book *The White Horses of the Camargue. Following pages:* Le Grau-du-Roi is the one and only commune in Gard to have access to the Mediterranean.

"We will always be small winemakers, who are close to their vines and their wines, so that we understand how everything works together, and can manage the wine, the vineyards, and all the vines ourselves. You have to be close in order to understand how it all works."
— Geoffroy d'Allenas, winegrower, Château-Bas D'Aumelas

In the Languedoc region, daily activities range from chatting in the streets of Arles to sailing to kayaking in the Gorges du Tarn.

"Think Mediterranean fish with the salty whites, country lamb with fresh herbs with the luscious reds of summer vegetables with the region's fruit-forward rosés." — Enrica Bernardo

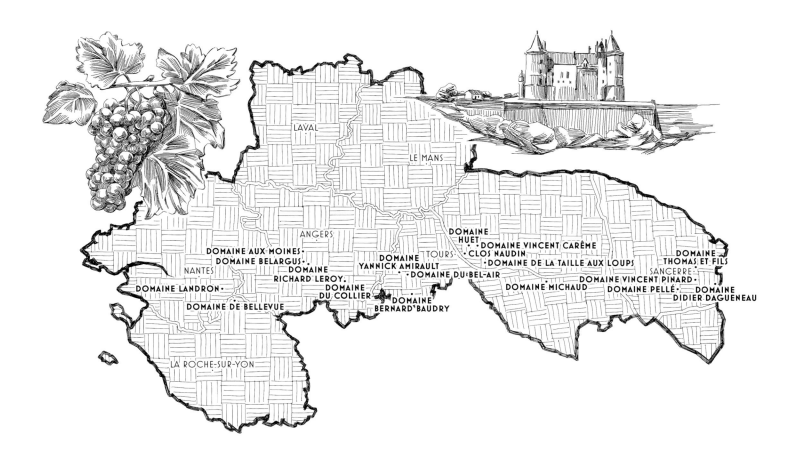

PAYS DE LA LOIRE

The most striking visual aspect of the Loire River valley winelands is the light that falls from vast skies looming over the gently rolling hillside vineyards. The vines themselves seem to join heaven and earth, plunging their roots deep down into the soil while gazing skyward. We, too, find ourselves standing on the ground here, gazing upward into infinite space. I am not surprised to have met so many winegrowers in the Loire country who are acutely sensitive to ecological concerns, climate change, the living world on which their work depends. The precepts underlying their approach to maintaining high quality in their wines are incontestable: protection of the entire plant, biodynamic cultivation with the most minimal intervention in the vineyard possible, infinite variations on supporting symbiosis among multiple environmental factors. That Loire light seems to lend a gleam to the region's wines as much as it illuminates the winemaker's thinking. Loire winegrowers are serene, completely in sync with their art, unruffled by any need to prove themselves or to compete. Exchanging views with these winemakers reveals their rich diversity of approach, intellectual honesty and determined commitment to sustainable polyculture and to a luscious palate and maximum energy in their wines. Taken together, these qualities constitute a strong and noble farming culture. To travel through the Loire wine country is to encounter a perfect conjunction of human effort and nature.

Over the last twenty years, Domaine Frédéric Mabileau has become a pioneer of biodynamic and organic viticulture, as well as one of the greatest producers of Cabernet Franc. *Following pages:* With its distinctive Renaissance style, the Château de Chambord, in the Loire Valley, is one of the most recognizable castles in the world.

Muscadet, Anjou, Vouvray, Sancerre, Savennières: so many luminous wines, never heavy, and all the more worthwhile discovering given their exemplary price-to-quality ratio. The terroir varies greatly along the Loire River: the vineyards around Nantes, near the Atlantic, produce saline, lively and mineral muscadet; while Sancerre, far inland, is known for its delicate pinot noir and aromatic sauvignon blanc. In between lie the sharply defined dry chenin blanc of Savennières and the extraordinary sweet wines of Vouvray and Layon. Master makers of these dessert wines in recent years include Philippe Foreau of Domaine du Clos Naudin, in Vouvray; and Patrick Baudouin at his eponymous estate and Philippe and Catherine Delesvaux at theirs, both in Layon. Between the splendid cities of Anjou and Tours, we pass through the triangular heart of top-notch cabernet franc–growing country, where charming wines are made in the Saumur-Champigny, Chinon, Bourgueil and Saint-Nicolas-de-Bourgueil AOCs. The cellars here, dug deep into the tuffeau, are impressive, and so naturally humid that ullage (topping up the casks during barrel aging to compensate for the evaporated "angel's share") is rarely necessary.

Among the Loire's several superb wines, a few finds stand out. The Muscadet AOC has in the last few years seen a spectacular improvement in quality. Fans of a respectfully ecological approach will not be disappointed by the work of Jo Landron, at Domaines Landron, or Jérôme Bretaudeau, proprietor of Domaine de Bellevue— whose wines are among the real jewels of this campaign of renewal. Bretaudeau's story is like a fairy tale. He discovered the world of wine by accident, at age twelve, thanks to a book about the world's best wines that he just devoured, finding his vocation in the process. Early in his career, as the prices of grand cru vintages were climbing and he could no longer afford them, Bretaudeau turned to the Loire Valley, where he met local winegrowers, discussed their metier with them and fell in love with their wines, though these were not of wide interest in the 1990s. After completing his oenological training at age

Inside Château de Beauregard, which has been classified as a historical monument since 1840.   201

The Loire Valley is known for its Renaissance châteaux, most of which are in the towns of Amboise, Angers, Blois, Chinon, Orléans and Tours. *Following pages, from left:* From the beginning of the spring season to the end of the fall, the Château de Chambord hosts equestrian demonstrations for guests to enjoy; intricate Renaissance details at Château de Chambord.

"Loire wines have an incredible quality. The region is known for dry whites. They have freshness in the mouth, a controlled acidity, subtle, tasty notes, salt... But if you like Pinot Noir, there are also extraordinary red Sancerres."

—Pascaline Lepeltier, 2018's Best Sommelier of France and Loire Valley native

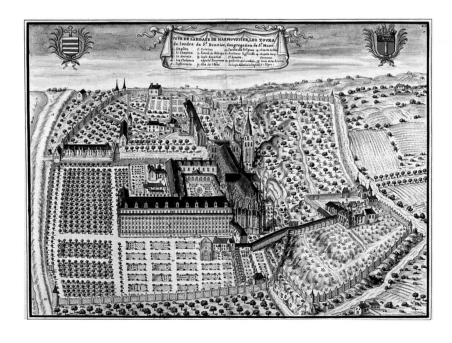

twenty-six, he purchased two hectares (five acres) of vineyard in Gétigné in 2001, which he gradually expanded to twenty hectares (fifty acres). For Bretaudeau, the wine-growing world constitutes a single family whose members all understand one another, because they speak the same language. For him, research and experimentation fuse together to marvelous effect. Today, each wine he releases is even better than the last, and they are found on the finest gastronomic tables and in the cellars of the most informed collectors worldwide. For me, Bretaudeau exemplifies what a winegrower can do when he focuses his efforts on remaining always in harmony with nature while seeking out ever-new experiences.

As I say of Corsica: discover, or rediscover, the wines of the Loire, where you are sure to find wonders created by winegrowers of talent and full of passion, and you will not be disappointed. The cuvées that express the soul of the Loire's Atlantic terroir are distinguished, elegant, mouthwatering, and the choice is wide, ranging from the vibrant wines grown around Nantes to the luminous vintages of Anjou, to the delectable wines of Savennières. The inland vineyards express a riverine soul—and not only of the Loire itself, but of its tributaries, the Allier, Cher, Indre, Loir, Sèvre Nantaise and Vienne—revealed in the aristocratic wines of Layon, Saumur and Chinon; the intriguing wines of Bourgueil; Vouvray's and Montlouis's vintages, at once tender and lively; and the sapid, exciting flavors of Sancerre. Again, the choice is wide, but all these terroirs have one thing in common: power, a structure notable less for its roundness than for its length, depth and a thrilling intensity. For these are wines fed by a perfectly balanced triad of air, sky and water in a land that really does seem to have been blessed by the gods. In the Loire Valley, we cannot forget that it was here, all along the river, that the kings of France once built their castles. Surrounded by such a majestic heritage, in the heart of much-cherished and welcoming landscapes, you are sure to find contentment.

Seafood and locally made products can be savored on and off the water around the Loire Valley. *Following pages, from left:* Taking care of the garden in the summer months; Château de la Bourdaisière owner Prince Louis-Albert De Broglie, also known as "Le Prince Jardinier" or "The Gardening Prince."

A group of coopers works in Tours, in 1895.

"I thought it would be nice to wake this sleeping beauty by making it a laboratory for my convictions."

— Prince Louis-Albert de Broglie, owner of Château de la Bourdaisière

Wine tasting and exploring the lush and vibrant landscapes (and interiors) of the Loire Valley.

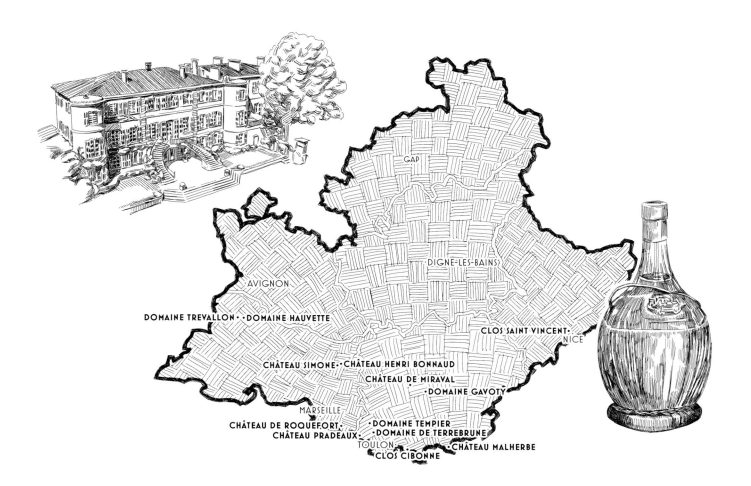

PROVENCE

———◆———

Provence is a place for vacations in the sun, both on its famous coasts and in its less-well-known but attractive backcountry. From Les Baux-de-Provence to the Alps to the seacoast, Provence is bursting with postcard-pretty landscapes. In terms of wine, the region is too often thought of in only one hue: rosé. To be sure, some Provençal rosés can pleasantly surprise you: the Cinsault and tibouren varietals yield aromatic, floral, subtle, light wines well suited to summertime dining. In vineyards lying in the inland zone running from Aix-en-Provence to Avignon and on to Saint-Tropez, you can find lovely rosés whose high quality is due to the winegrowers' respect for their terroir and the human scale of production.

I invite you to rediscover the land made famous by Marcel Pagnol, the novelist and filmmaker who did so much to define our image of his native Provence, with its melodic Italianate language and accent and its atmosphere heady with the scents of the southern Mediterranean. In Bandol, whose hill-ringed bay is like a natural amphitheater open to the sea, you find top-notch reds made from mourvèdre, a grape that dislikes damp weather and is thus perfectly adapted to the Mediterranean climate. In its youth, mourvèdre is structured, viscous, sometimes a touch rustic, even rough-edged. Yet it ages very well and, like most great wines, develops pronounced delicacy and lightness with time. Here, Domaine Tempier is a recognized institution that has

"*Provence: One of the most desirable places to inhabit in the world—lush vineyards, olive groves, oak, pine, and plane trees that dominate the Medieval villages, and good cheap wine.*"

—*Susana Iwase Hanson, founder of Provence Living Consulting*

inspired other estates to strive to improve their offerings. Savoring a mature Bandol can be a real thrill, especially when paired with, say, squab stuffed with black truffles from the Provençal Alps.

Dominique Hauvette, in Les Baux-de-Provence, makes extraordinary white wines, dynamic, full of character, with a chiseled profile, and mouthwatering. These are wines with strong personalities that evoke strong feelings, a delight for the gastronome, especially accompanying a fillet of fresh-caught red mullet cooked with a sprig of thyme and served with a vegetable confit. Since her debut as a winemaker, Hauvette has been a devotee of an authentically Provençal approach. Other notable whites include those made in the Cassis AOC; their discreet iodine note is a terrific match for a simple feast of raw sea urchins. North of Nice, the Bellet appellation highlights rolle (a varietal we have already encountered in Corsica—see above), the greatest Mediterranean wine grape, which yields perfumed whites, succulent and with a certain jovial character.

The area around Aix-en-Provence, plus two nearby villages, Meyreuil and Le Tholonet, which all together comprise the tiny Palette AOC (with just 45 hectares/111 acres of vineyards), is worth noting. One historic domaine, Château Simone, fought hard for more than a century to secure the AOC's recognition, supported by a few others, such as Château Henri Bonnaud. Today, Palette produces some of the Mediterranean's greatest whites. Its signature blends are luscious and direct, with very good aging potential.

Because its most outstanding wines are still largely unknown, while its quasi-industrial production of simple quaffing wines is often deprecated, Provence offers the potential for the kinds of discoveries wine lovers often dream of. Here, with a little bit of patience and attention, the curious visitor cannot help but find cause for delight.

The majestic entrance of Château de la Messardière, a nineteenth-century castle above the gulf of Saint-Tropez. *Following pages, from left:* Homemade pesto and a garden party lunch tablescape, both photographed by Jamie Beck for her book *An American in Provence: Art, Life and Photography.*

Strolling in the sun, reading, dining, and tasting wine in the Provençal paradise. *Following pages, from left:* Fresh tomatoes from the garden and olive oil for a delicious, healthy midday snack in nature; lunch in Aix-en-Provence.

"Nature in Provence is everything. It is what gives us the unbelievably incredible food ingredients sold at local farmer's markets, the flowers, the wine, the bees, and butterflies. It's all completely connected here and surrounds you in a way that folds you in."

— Jamie Beck, author

"We want to really give the quintessence of the terroirs because there are many terroirs here: to give the quintessence of each terroir in each vintage."

— Laurent Fortin, managing director, Domaine de la Bégude

Home to more than four hundred wineries, Provence welcomes thousands of visitors to its best local vineyards each year. *Following pages, from left:* At family-run Domaine de la Begude, guests can taste the vineyard's collection of red, white, and rosé wines. Originally specializing in rosé, Provence has a millennium-old wine-growing history.

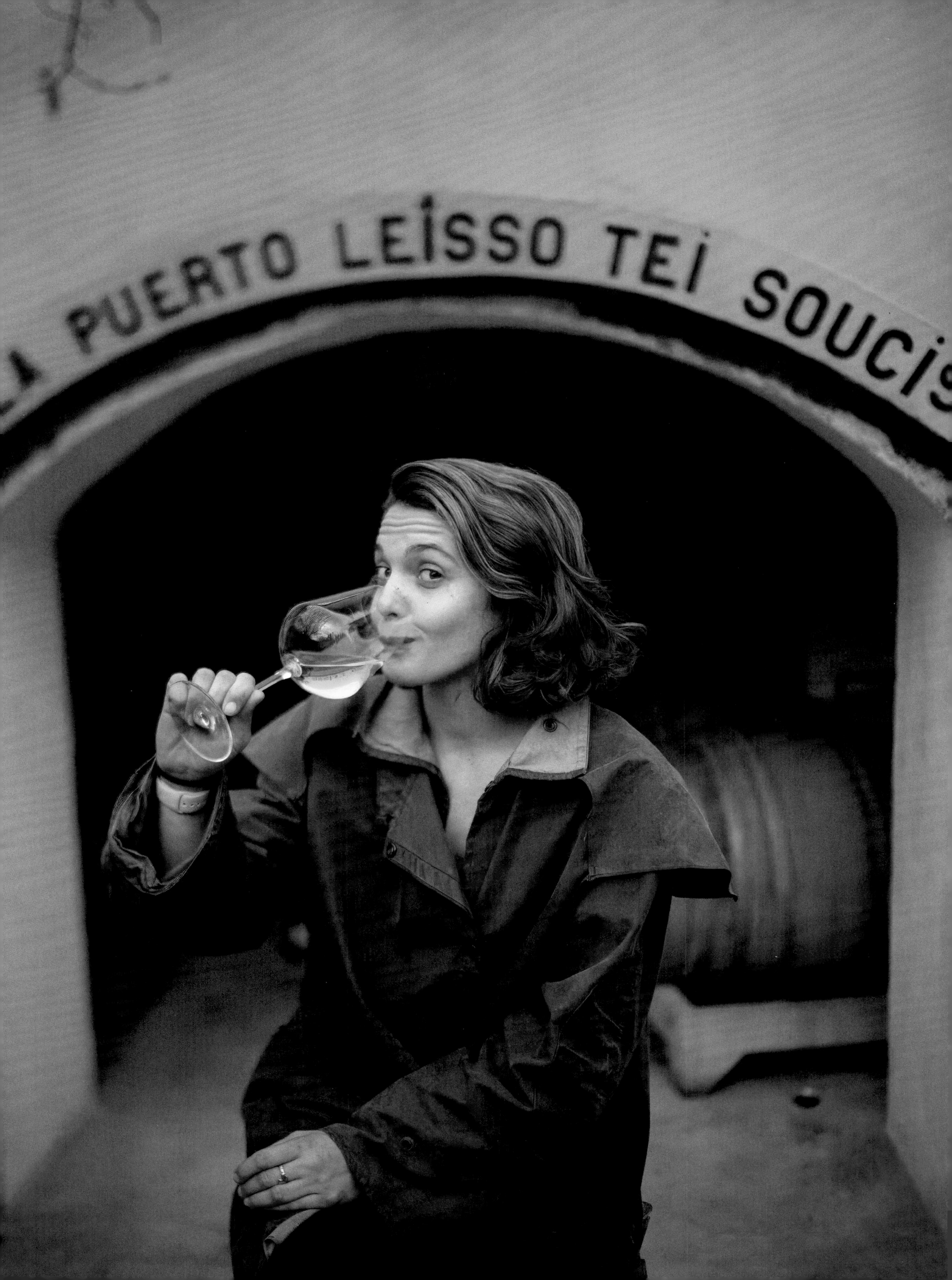
PUERTO LEISSO TEI SOUCIS

"No other wine region is so tied to the wonderful soft pink hues rosé lovers have come to love."

— *Laurie Forster, wine expert*

Staying at a *bastide* is part of the quintessential Provence experience. Specific to the South of France, they are large manor houses in the countryside. *Following pages, from left:* The Abbaye Notre-Dame de Sénanque, painted by Kristal Serna; a woman and her daughter in traditional clothing in Saint-Tropez.

When harvesting season starts at the end of August, Provence becomes even more magical.

"We don't buy a grape. We don't buy a liter. That's our philosophy. We are growers. We are not merchants."

— Daniel Brunier, winegrower, Domaine du Vieux Télégraphe

Post-dinner sweet treats with local wine at Château de Peyrassol. *Opposite:* Within thirteen hectares of parasol pines, cypress trees, and fragrant jasmine, Château de la Messardière overlooks the French Riviera, making it a dreamy oasis in the heart of Saint-Tropez.

"Provence is something for all the senses—the sound of the cicadas, the deep blue sky against the dark green hills, the smell of rosemary and lavender, the wonderful food and the warmth of the sun on your face."

— Sue Aitken, founder of Boutique Provençale

From Saint-Jean-Cap-Ferrat to Cannes and from lunch to sunset, local Provencal wines are a sweet escape during hot summer days spent in the South of France.

SAVOY

When I tell you that Savoy's wines are born near the Alps, dominated by Mont Blanc, you might suspect that I lack confidence in your knowledge of French geography. But when I add that these wines are endowed with the character of the region's inhabitants and of the mountains that loom over its vineyards, perhaps you'll find my judgment less banal. While the tradition of winemaking here is of course not as old as the hills—or rather, the mountains—Savoy's wines have been known and appreciated since antiquity. Like the Savoyards themselves, the region's wines have an austere side, upright and reserved—they can be a little hard to get to know. In the mouth, you find a truly alpine verticality, with a markedly saline and acid-driven finish. Yet today Savoyard wine is still too often dismissed for its (unbeatable) entry-level pricing and its too-easy association with a single image: après-ski fondue parties.

In fact, Savoy offers real finds made from indigenous varietals. With Mont Blanc towering above, local families work to preserve the unique spirit of their mountain terroir, in vineyards ranging from very steep to gently sloping. I can think of only one way to describe that spirit: the very soul of altitude.

In viticulture, mountains and forests are influences as important as ocean air, Mediterranean sun or a cooling river. A mountainous terroir affects the weather above all by creating a wide temperature range (both

"The word freshness could be considered just a polite way to describe high acidity, and yet this seems the most apt single word to describe French Alpine wines."

— Wink Lorch, author of Wines of the French Alps

daily and seasonal), which enables the winegrower to obtain optimal maturity of grape skins and seeds, the essential factor in developing a complex nose and silky tannins. Mountain wines are lively, vertical, appetizing, ideal matches for a variety of dishes. They tend to be uncompromising, and opinions about them may be divided, since some are rugged, with the broad-shouldered profile typical of wines made far from the ocean, and even a Nordic forthrightness. At their best, high-altitude wines are both broad and long, serious and dependable, balancing viscosity against freshness. Hot summers and cold winters lend them density. They open with a generous volume as charming as their sharply focused finish. In between, they are direct and linear, balanced and long. The wines of Savoy are endowed with an invigorating complexity; to be enjoyed at their best, they also really need to open out, and fortunately they can age well for ten years or more.

In this region, what with the cold, fog, snow and rain, sunshine is indispensable as it is perhaps nowhere else. The secret to success often lies in the terraced vineyards' southern exposure and an emphasis on old vines. Wine grapes are certainly capable of adapting to such intermittently extreme climatic conditions; like an acrobat, they may astonish us with the fragility, reserve and sophistication of the wines they yield. Savoyard wines demand an intellectual approach, with their refined silhouette and lovely crystalline purity. They lose their stern youthful severity with time, or when a warm and sunny vintage lends them extra fleshiness and charm. Their enduring freshness is the hallmark of their elegance and distinction, even nobility—all qualities that deserve our appreciation.

As you will have gathered by now, I believe that a winemaking tradition so venerable and so deeply embedded in its terroir, yet afflicted with such a biased image, deserves that we pause and ask the winegrowers themselves if the latest news is encouraging. It is. Here, as in the Loire Valley, a younger generation has rewritten the rules. Their dynamic approach is highlighting such local white varietals as roussette (aka altesse) and jacquère, among others. Through research and experimentation—pure trial and error—in techniques of élevage, these winemakers have succeeded in creating delicious mineral-driven wines that, while they retain a slightly angular rigor, also offer the discerning palate the luminous clarity of sunlight dancing on a mountain stream. These are substantial wines, dense, long, with a pleasing weight. They are excellent as an aperitif, and with freshwater fish or cheese—fine wines, well worth discovering.

Savoyard reds today can be a bit more rustic, peppery, with slightly astringent tannins—perfect for enjoyment in winter. The mondeuse grape in particular yields thick-textured juice with a tannic structure that hardly says "summer." Nonetheless, some winemakers here, as in Beaujolais, are striving to produce lighter styles that emphasize the fruit for its own sake, with supple, easy-drinking results.

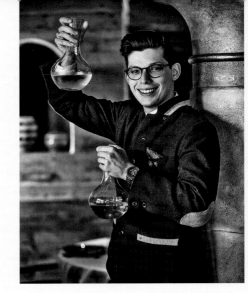

"Our vines grow in limestone scree soil, a preferred terroir for our different grape varieties where whites and reds blend harmoniously."

— Jean Vullien, winegrower, Domaine Jean Vullien

From harvesting grapes to making homemade cheese, the Savoy region is full of Alpine traditions and delicious products. *Following pages, from left:* A unique interpretation of the Galette des Rois, or Kings Cake, at Cheval Blanc Courchevel; the art of wine pairing at Airelles Courchevel.

The village of Seyssel also gives its name to a white wine appellation of the region. *Previous pages, from left to right:* Traditional cow bells made in the Savoy region, here on display at the Old Domancy craft festival; cows walk freely in nature on the pastures of Sainte-Foy-Tarentaise.

"Savoie is the most exciting wine region in the world!"
— Paul Einbund, owner, director, and sommelier, The Morris, San Francisco

The majestic views of the Savoy region will take away the breath of any visitor, whether staying in the valley or on the mountain. *Following pages:* At 1,100 meters in altitude, the hamlet of Chantemerle is one of the highest in Samoëns area.

Following pages, from left to right: Traditional details at La Bouitte, a gastronomical restaurant in Saint-Martin-de-Belleville; sharing dessert at Le Coucou Méribel.

A luxurious five-star hotel in the heart of Méribel, Le Coucou welcomes guests to its one-of-a-kind spa each winter season. *Opposite:* A large selection of cheeses, available for guests to savor at La Bouitte hotel and restaurant.

"Savoyard wines demand an intellectual approach, with their refined silhouette and lovely crystalline purity.

They lose their stern youthful severity with time, or when a warm and sunny vintage lends them extra fleshiness and charm."

— Enrico Bernardo

From the agriculture fair to the Retour des Alpages festival, the Savoy region is the host of many traditional celebrations that are still honored to this day. *Following pages, from left:* Overlooking the snowy Alpine landscapes from L'Apogée Courchevel, a unique destination in the heartland of Savoy dedicated to highly experienced skiers; the meandering mountain roads and snowy forests of Savoy.

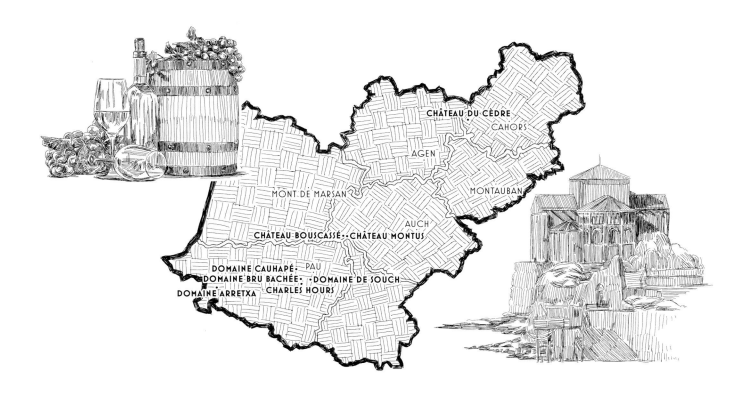

SOUTHWEST

France's southwestern wine-growing country has one great advantage, and one great disadvantage, of being quite remote from Paris. The disadvantage is that its wines remain somewhat unknown and undervalued among wine lovers. The advantage is that southwestern wines are the authentic products of indigenous varietals, grown in vineyards surrounded by tranquil wilderness.

The Southwest enjoys a second summer and gentle autumn weather that yield structured red wines that taste terrific with, say, a fine rib of beef. The warm harvest season, and a wide diurnal temperature shift due to dual influence of the Pyrenean foothills and the Atlantic, allows the local varietals, with their bold tannic structure, to ripen fully. Thus wines from the Cahors and Madiran AOCs offer both complexity and a chewy density. Cahors reds are made with côt—a grape more widely known today as malbec, the name given to the varietal in Argentina, where it arrived in the 1800s and has since found spectacular success. Madiran is made primarily from tannat, a highly tannic, even astringent grape, which has similarly been renamed harriague in Uruguay (after Pascual Harriague, a Basque winegrower who introduced it to South America around 1840). Both Madiran and red Cahors tend to require significant aging before they can be properly appreciated, given their great aromatic complexity and powerful character. Cahors reds are enchantingly

"The advantage is that southwestern wines are the authentic products of indigenous varietals, grown in vineyards surrounded by tranquil wilderness." —Enrico Bernardo

Made up of five subregions, the southwest of France is home to an array of different vineyards, as well as mountains and châteaux.

dense and rounded, with pastry notes—vanilla, licorice, blueberry. They are best enjoyed with friends over a cassoulet or other rich fare, like a gigot de sept heures (seven-hour roast lamb). Madiran, which I would nickname "hunter's wine," at twenty years old is a perfect match for partridge, truffled woodcock or even lièvre à la royale (whole hare braised in red wine and served with a sauce made from its heart, liver, lungs and blood). These are winter wines that cry out for long decanting and slow sipping by a hearth fire. What is more, both Cahors and Madiran offer an excellent price-to-quality ratio that ought to enable them to do well on the market once again.

The Southwest's other notable products are all sweet white wines from the Monbazillac, Pacherenc du Vic-Bilh and Jurançon AOCs, made from an array of exciting varietals, with gros manseng, courbu and petit courbu heading the list. In their dry versions, wines made from these grapes in these appellations are natural-born aperitifs that develop smoky notes with age. They offer an attractive verticality and great aromatic intensity, elegant, precise and mineral. In their sweet versions, the same wines take on notes of tropical fruit such as pineapple, as well as almond and dried apricot. They pair well with desserts or pastries—think orange soufflé or apricot tart. They are also good with cheeses, especially Ossau-Iraty, king of the Basque dairy: the mingling of sweet and salty is just lovely, with a lingering finish.

In the Pyrenees, the Irouléguy appellation stands out, with its terraced cultivation and a microclimate protected by the mountains from the northern and Atlantic winds. Irouléguy whites, made principally from courbu and petit manseng (sometimes blended), unite mountain stoniness with oceanic salinity, to bracing effect. The appellation's reds are also very interesting, strong and vigorous, and highly age-worthy as well, thanks to the solid tannic structure obtained by blending tannat, cabernet franc and cabernet sauvignon. Like the Basque people, these wines are indeed engaging and enchanting.

Beyond these subregions, the Southwest offers an impressively wide array of wines, from the Côtes du Marmandais AOC in the west (where the varietals grown are the same as those of Bordeaux, which lies adjacent) to the Cotes de Millau, the region's easternmost appellation, in the Aveyron department, where gamay flourishes. In between, many indigenous varietals are grown. Marcillac's fer servadou, for example, makes gratifyingly savory reds with notes of licorice and red fruit; Fronton's negrette offers an impressive color and a charming bouquet of violet and peony; and Gaillac's sparklers made from mauzac are a welcome surprise, with their exceptional finesse. Finally, the high caliber of the wines of the Saint-Mont AOC and the area's striking biodiversity provide a reassuring example of how the wine-growing world can remain authentic, simple and of great quality.

I can only invite all wine lovers to discover the beautiful wines of France's Southwest, which offer so much potential, made as they are from a multitude of native varietals grown in an equally varied array of soils. Many of these wines can benefit from significant aging in bottle. For so many reasons, I am convinced that this region's reputation is poised to rebound, and that its wines will once again enjoy the recognition they deserve.

Enjoying locally produced wine at sunset at Château Capitoul.

The Southwest region of France offers a large variety of outdoor treasures, from lush landscapes to pristine vineyards.

"I don't need extra attention; the truth is in the glass."

—Henri Ramonteu, winegrower, Domaine Cauhapé

"If you steep tea too long, you lose it. Balance and modest extraction are crucial to guard the nobility of the wine."

— Jean-Claude Berrouet, winegrower

Delectable cuisine, homemade sweet treats, and handmade bread accompany any Southwest wine to perfection. *Following pages, from left:* Candlelit dinner at Château de Gudanes, an eight-hundred-year-old castle brought back to life after twelve years of renovation; Château Monestier La Tour is nestled in an idyllic, serene landscape consisting of three islands of vines in Monestier and Saussignac.

A fun hot summer night spent in the vineyards of Château l'Hospitalet, a wine resort dedicated to the art of living. *Opposite:* An idyllic walk in nature at Château Arton.

Peaceful moments savoring the best of the Southwest terroir. *Following pages, from left:* At biodynamic property Château Monestier La Tour in the heart of Bergerac, the process of winemaking is done in a way that respects nature, genuinely reflecting the beauty of the terroir; sheep in pasture, in the Basque Country.

"I try to work as naturally as possible. It's healthy for wine and for life."

— Peio Espil, winegrower, Domaine Ilarria

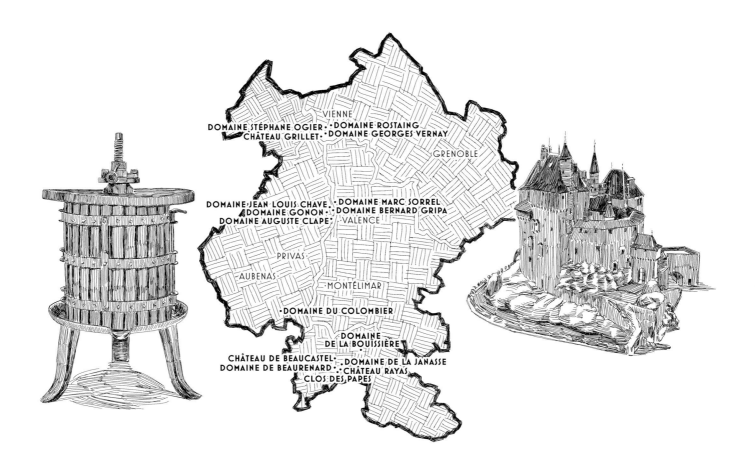

RHÔNE VALLEY

The Rhône Valley wine country reminds me of the Pays de la Loire. Both represent an alternative to the great regions of Burgundy and Bordeaux, and both are crossed by a great river. Like the Loire, the Rhône offers wine lovers not only true excellence but many outstanding values. The regions, of course, differ in some ways, too. The Atlantic blue of the skies over the Loire give way in the Rhône Valley to Mediterranean azure. Sun and wind always matter to wine growing, and the Mediterranean sun and winds are defining influences in Rhône vineyards. The region's spine is inevitably the river itself, running from north to south.

The Rhône Valley divides naturally into two distinct subregions. First comes the northern Rhône, whose limits are defined by the cities of Lyon and Montélimar. Here the estates are often spectacular, creating a very pretty landscape of curvilinear vineyards outlined by low stone walls on slopes rising steeply from the banks of the winding river as high as three hundred meters (nearly one thousand feet). Among them are terraced properties dating back to Gallo-Roman times so precipitous that no farm machinery can scale them. The soils, and their relationship to the region's cépages, are also of great interest. Syrah, the dominant red varietal, is planted in granitic or schistous terroirs. The Côte-Rôtie, Saint-Joseph, Hermitage and Cornas AOCs, as well as Seyssuel (vying for AOC status in recent years), produce wines with intense, persistent flavors. In the Côte-

Rôtie's two greatest terroirs, the schist-dominated soils of the Côte Brune confer black olive, pepper, iron, smoke and sanguine flavors, yet without rusticity or excess density; while the Côte Blonde's granite yields very refined, elegant and precise Syrahs with stimulating notes of violets and fruit—mulberry and blueberry. Considered together, these two soil types and the truly heroic efforts required to cultivate the Côte-Rôtie make for wines that are outstanding—if hard to find, given high demand and the tiny production of most of these estates.

Condrieu, just south of the Côte-Rotie, makes solely white wines from viognier, an aromatic varietal with floral and very charming tropical-fruit notes, ideal as an aperitif or paired with asparagus (notoriously hard to match with wine) or freshwater fish. In Saint-Joseph, Hermitage and Saint-Péray, two other white varietals dominate, marsanne and roussanne, which herald the Mediterranean with their notes of apricot, green olive, oregano and other aromatic herbs. These wines, luscious and fleshy on the palate, reveal their high quality in their food-friendly harmony of flavors. In the northern Rhône, to sum up, wine lovers will discover cuvées with a strong gastronomic aspect and a special succulence—commanding, fulsome, yet never heavy or too thick-textured.

As we head down into the southern Rhône, the river valley opens out and the landscape becomes more undulant. Here one major appellation stands out, curled within an extraordinary locale just north of Avignon: Châteauneuf-du-Pape. For a sommelier, this appellation's wines are like a canvas by Monet, bursting with nuance and color, yet all in perfect harmony. Châteauneuf-du-Pape displays richness, density and a trademark floral quality across an astoundingly diverse array of wines, made from no fewer than

The hilly landscape of the Bugey region, central in the Ain department.
Following pages, from left: Gazing over the Rhône Valley, the second-largest French region producer of AOC (or "Appellation d'Origine Contrôlée") wine after Bordeaux; the manicured garden of Château de Bagnols, located in the heart of the Beaujolais vineyards, nearby Lyon.

"Château Bois d'Arlène is a personal satisfaction to revive an old place, which has certainly been very important in the life and development of the region in the past."

— Philippe Bernard, manager and cellar master, Château Bois d'Arlène

Sunny relaxing moments at Château Bois d'Arlène and Domaine des Peyre.

"The more life there is, the healthier our vines will be. By maximizing life in our soils and in our vines, we act on the quality of our wines."
— Arthur Mazard, winegrower, Domaine Mazard

thirteen varietals grown in at least four distinctive soil types. In some parts of the AOC, the earth is carpeted with galets, rounded stones that reflect the sun while keeping the soil warm; elsewhere, sandy soils cool at night, yielding very light wines, floral, subtle, delicate, with a fine touch of acidity. In still other parts of the terroir we find clay or limestone. And while the region is very hot, it is always well ventilated. Winegrowers here get the most out of an ancient style of vine training called gobelet, which makes the vines resemble a chandelier. The result not only lends great natural beauty to the vineyard landscape but also helps the foliage canopy protect the grapes. Other inventive adaptations to the hot climate include, in some estates, allowing grass to grow at the foot of the vines to conserve moisture—a practice others entirely eschew, in order to protect the vines from competition with other plants. Another secret to this majestic terroir's success lies in its ancient vines, some a century old.

The Châteauneuf-du-Pape appellation covers a wide range of quality, from the banal to the exceptional. At their peak, the wines' perfect alchemy of force and finesse is astonishing, with a salinity on the palate married to warmth, roundness and great balance (and winemakers here are not afraid of alcohol, which can reach as high as 15.5 percent—without compromising the wines' equilibrium). As for the whites, despite amounting to only 7 percent of the AOC's production, they too are of exceptionally high quality, with a unique personality that has nothing to envy of the greatest whites made anywhere else on earth. Many of the appellations near Châteauneuf-du-Pape are well worth investigating, too, including Gigondas, Vacqueyras, Rasteau and Cairanne. Here you will find wines that afford great pleasure at reasonable prices—wines whose power may sometimes brush up against extravagance but that just as often make their mark with depth and poise.

For the wine lover eager for new discoveries, no other sun-soaked region offers such a mosaic of terroirs and grapes, an array that opens up a vast field of liberating possibilities. Is there some mystical influence exerted by the Palais des Papes in Avignon, the home of the papacy in exile in the fourteenth century? I do like to discern in Rhône wines a certain Catholic touch: spiritual inspiration, great capacity for aging (up to half a century) and a Mediterranean soulfulness. In the end, the Rhône Valley wines are like the people who live here: sunny, cheerful, welcoming. And like the speakers of the Rhône Valley's lilting Occitan dialects, these are wines that really sing.

From Lyon to Avignon, the Rhône Valley offers visitors tours and tastings at an array of estates that immerse guests in the rich local heritage. *Following pages, from left:* Tasting the Mont Ventoux black truffle. The Jaumard brothers, pictured here, have been working and roaming through their truffle fields for three generations; in Châteauneuf-du-Pape, Domaine Mazard is a family-run vineyard created by sixth-generation winegrowers.

"I was obsessed with Châteauneuf-du-Pape. I still am. In my family, Châteauneuf-du-Pape is the Pope of all wines."

— Isabel Ferrando, winegrower, Famille Isabel Ferrando

From poultry and truffle to specialty cheeses and chocolate, the Rhône Valley is full of gratifying local flavors.

GLOSSARY

APPELLATION D'ORIGINE CONTRÔLÉE (AOC)	"registered designation of origin": A certification of authenticity granted by France's Institut National de l'Origine et de la Qualité and designed to protect distinctive traditional regional agricultural products, including wine, based on the concept of terroir. There are more than 300 recognized AOCs. The AOC system is equivalent to the newer, EU-mandated appellation d'origine protégée ("protected designation of origin," AOP) system. However, French wine producers are permitted, and almost all prefer, to continue using the AOC terminology on their labels.
ASSEMBLAGE	The blending of wine from different grape varietals, vineyards, vintages, or crus prior to bottling in order to create a specific bouquet and flavor profile; the term refers to both the blending process and the resulting blend. The term assemblage is used especially in Bordeaux and Champagne.
BARRIQUE	An oak barrel or cask for aging wine after vinification and élevage and prior to bottling. Capacity varies greatly; in France, about 200 liters/53 U.S. gallons is typical.
BLANC DE BLANCS	"white from whites": Champagne made exclusively from white grapes, meaning chardonnay (or in very rare cases pinot blanc).
BLANC DE NOIRS	"white from blacks": Champagne made exclusively from the black grapes pinot noir and pinot meunier.
CÉPAGE	Wine grape variety (aka varietal). This term is sometimes also used as the equivalent of encepagement.
CLOS	An enclosed, usually walled, vineyard (or field or orchard). In Burgundy, clos are traditionally surrounded by distinctive drystone (mortarless) walls. Many Burgundian single-vineyard estates include the term clos in their name.
COTEAU	"hillside": A sloping vineyard, archetypally one that rises, gently or steeply, from a riverbank.
CRU	"growth": A vineyard or group of vineyards, especially one of recognized quality. In Champagne, the top level is grand cru, followed by premier cru. The famous classification of the Médoc estates on the Left Bank of the Garonne in Bordeaux into five numbered crus classés in 1855 resulted from the region's contribution to the Exposition Universelle in Paris in that year. The system has been adjusted very slightly only twice, in 1856 and 1973.
CRUS BOURGEOIS	In Bordeaux, a classification of Médoc wines immediately below the five 1855 crus classés and above the crus artisans (a 150-year-old classification officially restored by EU regulations in 1994). The crus bourgeois include about 250 estates. However, the use of this traditional term on wine labels since 2000 is confusing: In 2003–7, there were three levels of crus bourgeois; the terms were all abolished 2007–10; a single level was used 2010–20; in 2020, the old three-tier system was reintroduced. The three designations (cru bourgeois, cru bourgeois supérieur, cru bourgeois exceptionnel) are awarded annually upon application from the producer and announced about two years after the vintage.

CUVÉE	"vatful": A specific wine. Depending on context, this word can be in effect synonymous with the term vintage; assemblage/blend; or, for estates that release more than one wine, label. In Champagne, the word has a very special separate meaning: The cuvée is the juice rendered by an initial, gentle pressing of the grapes, amounting to the first 2,050 liters/542 U.S. gallons of juice from 4,000 kilograms/8,818 pounds of grapes, which produces the finest wine.
CUVERIE	The fermentation vats of a winery and the facilities that house them; the term can also be used as a metonym for winery.
DOMAINE	"estate": A winegrowing property, which may range from tiny to vast.
DOSAGE	In Champagne, dosage refers to the process of adding a small amount of sweetener (most often beet sugar) and reserve wine to top up each bottle after disgorgement (when the plug of lees accumulated in the neck of the bottle is removed) prior to corking, sealing, and release to market. Since the Champagne method's secondary fermentation in bottle normally converts all the wine's sugar into alcohol, dosage is the only way to control the level of sweetness and to balance the wine's acidity. The amount of residual sugar varies from 0 grams per liter for brut nature/brut zéro champagnes up to 50 grams or more for (now very rare) dessert champagnes, but 8–12 grams is typical.
ÉLEVAGE	"raising, bringing up" (as in rearing children or livestock): The progression of all the stages between fermentation and bottling, including aging (in vat, tank, barrel, amphora, etc.), fining, and filtering.
ENCEPAGEMENT	The relative proportions of the different grapes varieties grown in a single vineyard or on an entire estate, or of those used to make a particular blend. The term can also refer to grapes all of the same varietal but grown in different vineyards or in different vineyard parcels.
EN PRIMEUR	Essentially, "wine futures": A method of selling vintage wine while it is still in the barrel, usually 12 to 18 months prior to its official release. In France, this practice is most common in Bordeaux, Burgundy, and the Rhône Valley. Some collectors purchase en primeur to save money on wine they intend someday to drink; others, as an investment.
LIEU-DIT	"place called": A lieu-dit (also spelled lieudit) is any named but uninhabited locale, usually very small. As a means of designating vineyard locations, the term is structurally parallel to village. The names of most lieu-dits arose spontaneously, often centuries ago, among nearby villagers, drawing inspiration from such sources as local geography, history, and folklore. The term is especially important in Burgundian vineyard nomenclature.
MALOLACTIC CONVERSION	Sometimes also called "malolactic fermentation," this is the process through which the very tart-tasting malic acid naturally present in grapes is converted into milder-tasting lactic acid to produce a rounder, softer palate with greater body and persistence. Usually "malo" is induced as a secondary process in the vat immediately following the primary fermentation of grape must by the introduction of specific species of lactic acid bacteria, but it can be achieved during barrel aging instead. The process is conventionally used for most red wine production as well as for certain white wines, especially chardonnay.

MAQUIS	Maquis is dense scrubby vegetation comprising evergreen shrubs and small trees, characteristic of many Mediterranean coastal areas. The word maquis derives from the Corsican Italian dialect word macchia.
MILLÉSIME	"vintage"
MONOPOLE	"monopoly": In Burgundy, a monopole is any wine-growing area controlled by a single winery. It can be as small as a single vineyard or as large as an entire AOC.
SECOND WINE	Bordeaux to refer to a second-label wine made from cuvées not selected for use in the estate's grand vin (first label). Some producers also release a third or even a fourth wine.
SÉLECTION DE GRAINS NOBLES (SGN)	"selection of noble berries": This term designates wines made from grapes that the winegrower allows to become affected by the beneficial Botrytis cinerea fungus, aka "noble rot." In relatively dry conditions, the fungus partially dehydrates (raisinates) the grapes, concentrating their juice. The result is sweet dessert wines with rich, concentrated flavors. In France, the two most important regions producing SGN wines are Alsace and the Loire Valley.
SINGLE-VARIETAL	An unblended wine, one made from only a single grape variety. However, depending upon regional regulations in France, small amounts (sometimes up to fifteen percent or so) of other varietals are sometimes permitted without any requirement to note what is in effect a blend on the label.
SLOPE AND ASPECT	These terms define the steepness and the compass orientation (and hence the sun exposure and prevailing winds) of hillside or mountainside vineyards—critical aspects of terroir.
TERROIR	A given geographical area with specific environmental and human features that define an agricultural product's essential characteristics, including soil, topology, climate; farming and processing practices; and other aspects of traditional savoir-faire that contribute to the production of AOC products.
VIGNERON	"winegrower" and/or "winemaker"
VIN DU SIÈCLE	"wine of the century": A wine in fact determined to be from one of the best harvests of the previous decade. The designation is rarely awarded. In France during the twentieth century, a number of vins du siècle were declared most famously for the 1929, 1945, and 1961 vintages.
VIN MUTÉ	"silent wine": The term refers to the "silencing" (stopping) of the fermentation process by the addition of alcohol to fermenting must (juice) to preserve residual sugar. The method is similar to that used to make port. The method dates back to around 1300 in Roussillon, where vin muté is essentially synonymous with the term vin doux naturel (natural sweet wine).
VINTAGE	The year in which wine is produced.

ENRICO BERNARDO'S IDEAL WINE CELLAR

ALSACE

BAS-RHIN
DOMAINE BOEHLER
DOMAINE ÉTIENNE LOEW
DOMAINE MARC KREYDENWEISS
DOMAINE MÉLANIE PFISTER
DOMAINE OSTERTAG
DOMAINE VINCENT STOEFFLER

HAUT-RHIN
DOMAINE AGAPÉ
DOMAINE AGATHE BURSIN
DOMAINE ALBERT BOXLER
DOMAINE ALBERT MANN
DOMAINE ANDRÉ KIENTZLER
DOMAINE BARMÈS-BUECHER
DOMAINE DIRLER-CADÉ
DOMAINE DU CLOS SAINT-LANDELIN
     VÉRONIQUE ET THOMAS MURÉ
DOMAINE EMILE BEYER
DOMAINE FRANÇOIS SCHMITT
DOMAINE HENRY FUCHS & FILS
DOMAINE JEAN ET JEAN-LOUIS TRAPET
DOMAINE JEAN-MARC BERNHARD
DOMAINE JOSMEYER
DOMAINE KIRRENBOURG
DOMAINE LAURENT BARTH
DOMAINE LÉON BOESCH
DOMAINE MANN–VIGNOBLE DES 3
     TERRES
DOMAINE MARC TEMPÉ
DOMAINE MARCEL DEISS
DOMAINE MAURICE SCHOECH
DOMAINE MEYER-FONNÉ
DOMAINE PAUL BLANCK
DOMAINE PAUL GINGLINGER
DOMAINE SCHOFFIT
DOMAINE VALENTIN ZUSSLIN
DOMAINE WEINBACH
DOMAINE WEINZAEPFEL
DOMAINE ZINCK
DOMAINE ZIND HUMBRECHT
DOMAINES SCHLUMBERGER
JEAN-CLAUDE BUECHER & FILS
LÉON BEYER
MAISON TRIMBACH

BORDEAUX

BLAYE, BOURG, AND BORDEAUX
CHÂTEAU BEL-AIR LA ROYÈRE
CHÂTEAU MARTINAT
CHÂTEAU ROC DE CAMBES
CLOS DES LUNES

HAUT-MÉDOC, MOULIS, LISTRAC
CHÂTEAU BELGRAVE
CHÂTEAU BELLE-VUE
CHÂTEAU CANTEMERLE
CHÂTEAU CHASSE-SPLEEN
CHÂTEAU CLARKE
CHÂTEAU FOURCAS HOSTEN
CHÂTEAU LA LAGUNE
CHÂTEAU LA TOUR DE BY
CHÂTEAU LES ORMES SORBET
CHÂTEAU POUJEAUX
CHÂTEAU SOCIANDO-MALLET

LIBOURNAIS, CÔTES DE BORDEAUX
CHÂTEAU CANON PÉCRESSE
CHÂTEAU D'AIGUILHE
CHÂTEAU DE CARLES
CHÂTEAU FONTENIL
CHÂTEAU MOULIN PEY-LABRIE
CHÂTEAU SAMION
CHÂTEAU TOURNEFEUILLE
CLOS PUY ARNAUD
DOMAINE DE L'A
VIEUX CHÂTEAU SAINT-ANDRÉ

MARGAUX
CHÂTEAU BOYD-CANTENAC
CHÂTEAU BRANE-CANTENAC
CHÂTEAU CANTENAC BROWN
CHÂTEAU D'ISSAN
CHÂTEAU DAUZAC
CHÂTEAU DURFORT-VIVENS
CHÂTEAU FERRIÈRE
CHÂTEAU GISCOURS
CHÂTEAU KIRWAN
CHÂTEAU LABÉGORCE
CHÂTEAU LASCOMBES
CHÂTEAU MALESCOT SAINT-EXUPÉRY
CHÂTEAU MARGAUX
CHÂTEAU MARQUIS D'ALESME

CHÂTEAU MARQUIS DE TERME
CHÂTEAU MONBRISON
CHÂTEAU PALMER
CHÂTEAU PRIEURÉ-LICHINE
CHÂTEAU RAUZAN-SÉGLA

PAUILLAC
CHÂTEAU BATAILLEY
CHÂTEAU CLERC MILON
CHÂTEAU D'ARMAILHAC
CHÂTEAU DUHART-MILION
CHÂTEAU GRAND-PUY-LACOSTE
CHÂTEAU HAUT-BATAILLEY
CHÂTEAU LAFITE ROTHSCHILD
CHÂTEAU LATOUR
CHÂTEAU LYNCH-BAGES
CHÂTEAU MOUTON ROTHSCHILD
CHÂTEAU PIBRAN
CHÂTEAU PICHON BARON
CHÂTEAU PICHON LONGUEVILLE
     COMTESSE DE LALANDE
CHÂTEAU PONTET-CANET

PESSAC-LÉOGNAN, GRAVES
CHÂTEAU CARBONNIEUX
CHÂTEAU COUHINS-LURTON
CHÂTEAU DE FIEUZAL
CHÂTEAU HAUT-BAILLY
CHÂTEAU HAUT-BRION
CHÂTEAU LA MISSION HAUT-BRION
CHÂTEAU LARRIVET HAUT-BRION
CHÂTEAU LATOUR-MARTILLAC
CHÂTEAU LES CARMES DE HAUT-BRION
CHÂTEAU MALARTIC-LAGRAVIÈRE
CHÂTEAU OLIVIER
CHÂTEAU PAPE CLÉMENT
CHÂTEAU PEYRAT
CHÂTEAU SMITH HAUT LAFITTE
CLOS FLORIDÈNE
DOMAINE DE CHEVALIER

POMEROL
CHÂTEAU CERTAN DE MAY
CHÂTEAU CLINET
CHÂTEAU DE VALOIS
CHÂTEAU GAZIN
CHÂTEAU L'ÉGLISE-CLINET
CHÂTEAU L'ÉVANGILE
CHÂTEAU LA CONSEILLANTE

Sunset dinner on the lawn of Château de Bosgouet, in Normandy.

301

CHÂTEAU LA FLEUR-PÉTRUS
CHÂTEAU LA VIOLETTE
CHÂTEAU LAFLEUR
CHÂTEAU LATOUR À POMEROL
CHÂTEAU LE GAY
CHÂTEAU LE PIN
CHÂTEAU ROUGET
CHÂTEAU TROTANOY
CLOS DU CLOCHER
PETRUS
VIEUX CHÂTEAU CERTAN

SAINT-ÉMILION
CHÂTEAU ANGELUS
CHÂTEAU AUSONE
CHÂTEAU BEAU-SÉJOUR BÉCOT
CHÂTEAU BEAUSÉJOUR HÉRITIERS
    DUFFAU-LAGAROSSE
CHÂTEAU BÉLAIR-MONANGE
CHÂTEAU CANON
CHÂTEAU CANON-LA-GAFFELIÈRE
CHÂTEAU CHEVAL BLANC
CHÂTEAU CORBIN
CHÂTEAU FIGEAC
CHÂTEAU FONROQUE
CHÂTEAU GUADET
CHÂTEAU JEAN FAURE
CHÂTEAU LA CLOTTE
CHÂTEAU LA GAFFELIÈRE
CHÂTEAU LA MONDOTTE
CHÂTEAU LARCIS DUCASSE
CHÂTEAU PAVIE
CHÂTEAU PAVIE MACQUIN
CHÂTEAU ROCHEBELLE
CHÂTEAU TERTRE ROTEBOEUF
CHÂTEAU TROPLONG MONDOT
CHÂTEAU TROTTEVIEILLE
CHÂTEAU VALANDRAUD
CLOS FOURTET
CLOS SAINT-MARTIN

SAINT-ESTÈPHE
CHÂTEAU CALON SÉGUR
CHÂTEAU COS D'ESTOURNEL
CHÂTEAU COS LABORY
CHÂTEAU HAUT-MARBUZET
CHÂTEAU MONTROSE
CHÂTEAU ORMES DE PEZ
CHÂTEAU PHÉLAN SÉGUR

SAINT-JULIEN
CHÂTEAU BEYCHEVELLE
CHÂTEAU BRANAIRE-DUCRU
CHÂTEAU DUCRU-BEAUCAILLOU
CHÂTEAU GRUAUD LAROSE
CHÂTEAU LÉOVILLE BARTON

CHÂTEAU LÉOVILLE LAS CASES
CHÂTEAU LÉOVILLE POYFERRÉ
CHÂTEAU SAINT PIERRE
CHÂTEAU TALBOT
CLOS DU MARQUIS

SAUTERNES
CHÂTEAU CLIMENS
CHÂTEAU COUTET
CHÂTEAU D'YQUEM
CHÂTEAU DE FARGUES
CHÂTEAU DOISY-DAËNE
CHÂTEAU DOISY-VÉDRINES
CHÂTEAU GILETTE
CHÂTEAU GUIRAUD
CHÂTEAU LA TOUR BLANCHE
CHÂTEAU LAFAURIE-PEYRAGUEY
CHÂTEAU RAYMOND-LAFON
CHÂTEAU DE RAYNE VIGNEAU
CHÂTEAU RIEUSSEC
CHÂTEAU SIGALAS RABAUD
CHÂTEAU SUDUIRAUT

BURGUNDY

AUXEY-DURESSES, MONTHELIE, AND SAINT-ROMAIN
DOMAINE ALAIN GRAS
DOMAINE D'AUVENAY
DOMAINE ÉRIC DE SUREMAIN–CHÂTEAU
    DE MONTHELIE
DOMAINE HENRI ET GILLES BUISSON
DOMAINE JEAN ET GILLES LAFOUGE

BEAUJOLAIS
CHÂTEAU THIVIN
CLOS DE LA ROILETTE
DOMAINE MOREAU L'ARLESIENNE
DOMAINE CHERMETTE
DOMAINE DANIEL BOULAND
DOMAINE DE LA GROSSE PIERRE
DOMAINE DE LA MADONE
DOMAINE DES MARRANS
DOMAINE DES TERRES DORÉES
DOMAINE GEORGES DESCOMBES
DOMAINE JEAN FOILLARD
DOMAINE JEAN-MARC BURGAUD
DOMAINE JULES DESJOURNEYS
DOMAINE LABRUYÈRE
DOMAINE LAURENT MARTRAY
DOMAINE LOUIS CLAUDE DESVIGNES
DOMAINE MARCEL LAPIERRE
DOMAINE MERLIN
DOMAINE PAUL JANIN & FILS
DOMAINE THIBAULT LIGER-BELAIR

BEAUNE
DOMAINE ALBERT MOROT
DOMAINE DE BELLENE
DOMAINE DES CROIX
DOMAINE PHILIPPE PACALET
MAISON ALBERT BICHOT
MAISON JOSEPH DROUHIN
MAISON LOUIS JADOT

BOUZERON, RULLY
DOMAINE DE VILLAINE
DOMAINE DUREUIL-JANTHIAL
DOMAINE JEAN-BAPTISTE PONSOT
DOMAINE MICHEL BRIDAY
DOMAINE PAUL ET MARIE JACQUESON

CHABLIS
ALICE ET OLIVIER DE MOOR
DOMAINE BESSIN TREMBLAY
DOMAINE CHRISTIAN MOREAU PÈRE & FILS
DOMAINE COLINOT
DOMAINE D'HENRI
DOMAINE ELENI ET ÉDOUARD VOCORET
DOMAINE GABIN ET FÉLIX RICHOUX
DOMAINE GILBERT PICQ & SES FILS
DOMAINE GROSSOT
DOMAINE JEAN-PAUL & BENOÎT DROIN
DOMAINE LOUIS MICHEL & FILS
DOMAINE MOREAU-NAUDET
DOMAINE PASCAL RENAUD
DOMAINE PATTES LOUP
DOMAINE RAVENEAU
DOMAINE ROLAND LAVANTUREUX
DOMAINE VINCENT DAUVISSAT
DOMAINE WILLIAM FÈVRE

CHAMBOLLE-MUSIGNY
DOMAINE AMIOT-SERVELLE
DOMAINE COMTE GEORGES DE VOGÜÉ
DOMAINE FELETTIG
DOMAINE GEORGES ROUMIER
DOMAINE GHISLAINE BARTHOD
DOMAINE HUDELOT-NOËLLAT
DOMAINE JACQUES-FRÉDÉRIC MUGNIER

CHASSAGNE-MONTRACHET
DOMAINE ARMAND HEITZ
DOMAINE BACHELET-RAMONET
DOMAINE BENOÎT MOREAU
DOMAINE BERNARD MOREAU ET FILS
DOMAINE BRUNO COLIN
DOMAINE CAROLINE MOREY
DOMAINE FONTAINE-GAGNARD
DOMAINE LAMY-CAILLAT
DOMAINE MOREY-COFFINET

DOMAINE PAUL PILLOT
DOMAINE RAMONET
DOMAINE VINCENT DANCER

CHOREY-LES-BEAUNE , SAVIGNY-LÈS-BEAUNE
DOMAINE CHANDON DE BRIAILLES
DOMAINE JEAN-MARC & HUGUES PAVELOT
DOMAINE MICHEL ÉCARD
DOMAINE SERRIGNY
DOMAINE SIMON BIZE & FILS
DOMAINE SYLVAIN LOCHET
DOMAINE TOLLOT-BEAUT ET FILS

FIXIN
DOMAINE BERTHAUT-GERBET
DOMAINE PIERRE GELIN

GEVREY-CHAMBERTIN
DOMAINE ARMAND ROUSSEAU
DOMAINE BERNARD DUGAT-PY
DOMAINE CLAUDE DUGAT
DOMAINE DENIS BACHELET
DOMAINE DENIS MORTET
DOMAINE DROUHIN-LAROZE
DOMAINE DUROCHÉ
DOMAINE ESMONIN SYLVIE
DOMAINE FOURRIER
DOMAINE HENRI REBOURSEAU
DOMAINE HUMBERT FRÈRES
DOMAINE JEAN TRAPET PÈRE & FILS
DOMAINE JÉRÔME GALEYRAND
DOMAINE JOSEPH ROTY
DOMAINE LIPPE BOILEAU
DOMAINE LUCIEN BOILLOT & FILS
DOMAINE PERNOT PÈRE & FILS
DOMAINE PHILIPPE CHARLOPIN-PARIZOT
DOMAINE PIERRE DAMOY
DOMAINE ROSSIGNOL-TRAPET
DOMAINE SÉRAFIN PÈRE & FILS
DOMAINE THIERRY MORTET

GIVRY
DOMAINE DU CELLIER AUX MOINES
DOMAINE DU CLOS SALOMON
DOMAINE FRANÇOIS LUMPP
DOMAINE JOBLOT

HAUTES-CÔTES DE BEAUNE
DOMAINE ALEXANDRE PARIGOT
DOMAINE BORIS CHAMPY
DOMAINE FRANÇOIS D'ALLAINES

HAUTES-CÔTES DE NUITS
DOMAINE DAVID DUBAND
DOMAINE HOFFMANN-JAYER

DOMAINE NAUDIN-FERRAND
DOMAINE NICOLAS FAURE
DOMAINE VINCENT LEGOU

MÂCON, POUILLY-FUISSÉ, SAINT-VÉRAN
CHÂTEAU DES QUARTS
CLOS DES VIGNES DU MAYNES
DOMAINE BARRAUD
DOMAINE DE LA BONGRAN
DOMAINE DES HÉRITIERS DU COMTE LAFON
DOMAINE ÉRIC FOREST
DOMAINE FRANTZ CHAGNOLEAU
DOMAINE GUFFENS-HEYNEN
DOMAINE GUILLOT-BROUX
DOMAINE J.-A. FERRET
DOMAINE JACQUES SAUMAIZE
DOMAINE LA SOUFRANDIÈRE
DOMAINE MERLIN
DOMAINE ROBERT-DENOGENT
DOMAINE SAUMAIZE-MICHELIN
DOMAINE THIBERT PÈRE & FILS
DOMAINE VALETTE

MARANGES
DOMAINE CHEVROT ET FILS
DOMAINE NICOLAS PERRAULT

MARSANNAY
DOMAINE BART
DOMAINE BERNARD COILLOT PÈRE & FILS
DOMAINE BRUNO CLAIR
DOMAINE JEAN-MARIE FOURRIER
DOMAINE RENÉ BOUVIER
DOMAINE SYLVAIN PATAILLE

MERCUREY
DOMAINE FRANÇOIS RAQUILLET
DOMAINE JEANNIN-NALTET
DOMAINE LORENZON
DOMAINE MICHEL JUILLOT
DOMAINE THEULOT JUILLOT
DOMAINE VINCENT & JEAN-PIERRE CHARTON

MEURSAULT
ANTOINE JOBARD
DOMAINE ALBERT GRIVAULT
DOMAINE BALLOT-MILLOT
DOMAINE BERNARD MILLOT
DOMAINE BERTHELEMOT
DOMAINE BUISSON BATTAULT
DOMAINE BUISSON-CHARLES
DOMAINE COCHE-DURY
DOMAINE DES COMTES LAFON
DOMAINE HENRI BOILLOT
DOMAINE HENRI GERMAIN ET FILS

DOMAINE JACQUES PRIEUR
DOMAINE JEAN JAVILLIER & FILS
DOMAINE MATROT
DOMAINE MICHEL BOUZEREAU ET FILS
DOMAINE PIERRE MOREY
DOMAINE RÉMI JOBARD
DOMAINE ROULOT
DOMAINE SÉBASTIEN MAGNIEN
DOMAINE TESSIER
DOMAINE XAVIER MONNOT
MAISON VINCENT GIRARDIN

MONTAGNY
DOMAINE ALINE BEAUNÉ
DOMAINE BERTHENET
DOMAINE MAXIME COTTENCEAU
DOMAINE STÉPHANE ALADAME

MOREY-SAINT-DENIS
CLOS DE TART
DOMAINE ARLAUD
DOMAINE CASTAGNIER
DOMAINE CÉCILE TREMBLAY
DOMAINE DES BEAUMONT
DOMAINE DUJAC
DOMAINE HUBERT LIGNIER
DOMAINE LIGNIER-MICHELOT
DOMAINE PERROT-MINOT
DOMAINE PONSOT
DOMAINE ROBERT GROFFIER PÈRE & FILS
DOMAINE TAUPENOT-MERME
DOMAINES DES LAMBRAYS
LAURENT PONSOT

NUITS-SAINT-GEORGES
DOMAINE CHANTAL LESCURE
DOMAINE CHEVILLON-CHEZEAUX
DOMAINE DE L'ARLOT
DOMAINE DE LA VOUGERAIE
DOMAINE FAIVELEY
DOMAINE HENRI GOUGES
DOMAINE JEAN-MARC MILLOT
DOMAINE LÉCHENEAUT
DOMAINE MICHÈLE ET PATRICE RION
DOMAINE PRIEURÉ ROCH
DOMAINE ROBERT CHEVILLON
DOMAINE THIBAULT LIGER-BELAIR
MAISON MARCHAND-TAWSE

PERNAND-VERGELESSES, ALOXE-CORTON, LADOIX-SERRIGNY
DOMAINE BONNEAU DU MARTRAY
DOMAINE FOLLIN ARBELET
DOMAINE MICHEL MALLARD ET FILS
DOMAINE POISOT PÈRE & FILS
DOMAINE RAPET PÈRE & FILS

POMMARD

DOMAINE A.-F. GROS

DOMAINE DE COURCEL

DOMAINE DU COMTE ARMAND–LE CLOS
  DES ÉPENEAUX

DOMAINE JEAN MARC BOILLOT

DOMAINE VIOLOT-GUILLEMARD

DOMAINE Y. CLERGET

PULIGNY-MONTRACHET

DOMAINE ALAIN CHAVY

DOMAINE ÉTIENNE SAUZET

DOMAINE FRANCOIS CARILLON

DOMAINE JACQUES CARILLON

DOMAINE LEFLAIVE

DOMAINE THOMAS-COLLARDOT

SAINT-AUBIN

DOMAINE HENRI PRUDHON

DOMAINE HUBERT LAMY

DOMAINE JOSEPH COLIN

DOMAINE LARUE

DOMAINE MARC COLIN ET FILS

DOMAINE MOINGEON ANDRÉ ET FILS

JEAN CLAUDE BACHELET

PIERRE-YVES COLIN-MOREY

SANTENAY

DOMAINE ANNE-MARIE ET JEAN-MARC
  VINCENT

DOMAINE FRANÇOISE & DENIS CLAIR

DOMAINE JACQUES GIRARDIN

DOMAINE LUCIEN MUZARD & FILS

VOLNAY

DOMAINE DE LA POUSSE D'OR

DOMAINE DE MONTILLE

DOMAINE JEAN-MARC ET THOMAS BOULEY

DOMAINE MARQUIS D'ANGERVILLE

DOMAINE MICHEL LAFARGE

DOMAINE NICOLAS ROSSIGNOL

DOMAINE ROBLET-MONNOT

VOSNE-ROMANÉE

DOMAINE ANNE GROS

DOMAINE ARNOUX-LACHAUX

DOMAINE BIZOT

DOMAINE BRUNO CLAVELIER

DOMAINE CONFURON-COTETIDOT

DOMAINE DE LA ROMANÉE-CONTI

DOMAINE DU COMTE LIGER-BELAIR

DOMAINE ÉDOUARD CONFURON

DOMAINE EMMANUEL ROUGET

DOMAINE FRANÇOIS CONFURON-GINDRE

DOMAINE GEORGES MUGNERET-GIBOURG

DOMAINE JEAN GRIVOT

DOMAINE JEAN TARDY & FILS

DOMAINE LEROY

DOMAINE SYLVAIN CATHIARD & FILS

GÉRARD MUGNERET

MÉO-CAMUZET

VOUGEOT

CHÂTEAU DE LA TOUR

DOMAINE CHRISTIAN CLERGET

CHAMPAGNE

CÔTE DE SÉZANNE

DOMAINE COLLET

DOMAINE ULYSSE COLLIN

CÔTE DES BAR

CHAMPAGNE COESSENS

CHAMPAGNE DRAPPIER

CHAMPAGNE FLEURY

CHAMPAGNE HORIOT

CHAMPAGNE JACQUES LASSAIGNE

CHAMPAGNE MATHIEU

CHAMPAGNE PIERRE GERBAIS

CHAMPAGNE RÉMY MASSIN & FILS

CHAMPAGNE RUPPERT-LEROY

LES ROSES DE JEANNE

REMY LEROY

VOUETTE & SORBÉE

CÔTE DES BLANCS

CHAMPAGNE CAZALS CLAUDE

CHAMPAGNE DE SOUSA

CHAMPAGNE DELAMOTTE

CHAMPAGNE DUVAL-LEROY

CHAMPAGNE ETIENNE CALSAC

CHAMPAGNE GUIBORAT

CHAMPAGNE LANCELOT-PIENNE

CHAMPAGNE PASCAL AGRAPART

CHAMPAGNE PASCAL DOQUET

CHAMPAGNE PERTOIS-MORISET

CHAMPAGNE PHILIPPE LANCELOT

CHAMPAGNE PIERRE GIMONNET & FILS

CHAMPAGNE PIERRE MONCUIT

CHAMPAGNE R. & L. LEGRAS

CHAMPAGNE SALON

CHAMPAGNE VAZART-COQUART & FILS

CHAMPAGNE VEUVE FOURNY & FILS

DE SAINT-GALL

DIEBOLT-VALLOIS

DOMAINE DHONDT-GRELLET

DOMAINE DOYARD

DOMAINE JACQUES SELOSSE

LARMANDIER-BERNIER

PIERRE PÉTERS

SUENEN

MONTAGNE DE REIMS

ADRIEN RENOIR

BENOÎT LAHAYE

BERNARD BRÉMONT

CHAMPAGNE ANDRÉ CLOUET

CHAMPAGNE BÉRÈCHE & FILS

CHAMPAGNE BRUNO PAILLARD

CHAMPAGNE GEORGES REMY

CHAMPAGNE HENRIOT

CHAMPAGNE HUGUES GODMÉ

CHAMPAGNE HURÉ FRÈRES

CHAMPAGNE J. M. GOULARD

CHAMPAGNE LA CLOSERIE–JÉRÔME PRÉVOST

CHAMPAGNE MAILLY

CHAMPAGNE MARGUET

CHAMPAGNE MOUZON LEROUX & FILS

CHAMPAGNE NICOLAS MAILLART

CHAMPAGNE PALMER & CO

CHAMPAGNE PIERRE PAILLARD

CHAMPAGNE PLOYEZ-JACQUEMART

CHAMPAGNE RODEZ

CHAMPAGNE ROGER COULON

CHAMPAGNE SAVART

CHAMPAGNE TAITTINGER

CHAMPAGNE VILMART & CIE

CHAMPAGNE YANN ALEXANDRE

CHARLES HEIDSIECK

CHARTOGNE-TAILLET

DAVID LÉCLAPART

EGLY-OURIET

EMMANUEL BROCHET

FRANCIS BOULARD

G. H. MUMM

KRUG

LOUIS ROEDERER

RUINART

VEUVE CLICQUOT

VALLÉE DE LA MARNE

AR LENOBLE

CHAMPAGNE A. BERGÈRE

CHAMPAGNE ALFRED GRATIEN

CHAMPAGNE APOLLONIS–MICHEL LORIOT

CHAMPAGNE BILLECART-SALMON

CHAMPAGNE BOIZEL

CHAMPAGNE BOLLINGER

CHAMPAGNE CHRISTOPHE MIGNON

CHAMPAGNE DEHOURS

CHAMPAGNE DEUTZ

CHAMPAGNE FRANÇOISE BEDEL

CHAMPAGNE GEORGES LAVAL

CHAMPAGNE GONET-MÉDEVILLE

CHAMPAGNE GOSSET

CHAMPAGNE HENRI GIRAUD

CHAMPAGNE JACQUESSON

CHAMPAGNE JESTIN

CHAMPAGNE LAHERTE FRÈRES

CHAMPAGNE MARC HÉBRART

CHAMPAGNE POL ROGER

CHAMPAGNE R. POUILLON & FILS

CHAMPAGNE RÉGIS POISSINET

CHAMPAGNE RENÉ GEOFFROY

CHAMPAGNE TARLANT

DOM PÉRIGNON

FAMILLE MOUSSÉ

FRANCK PASCAL

JM SÉLÈQUE

LAURENT-PERRIER

LECLERC BRIANT

MOËT & CHANDON

PERRIER-JOUËT

PHILIPPONNAT

CORSICA

CANTINA DI TORRA–
NICOLAS MARIOTTI BINDI

CASTELLU DI BARICCI

CLOS CANARELLI

CLOS CANERECCIA

CLOS CULOMBU

CLOS D'ALZETO

CLOS LANDRY

CLOS NICROSI

CLOS SIGNADORE

CLOS VENTURI

DOMAINE 'ALZIPRATU

DOMAINE A PERACCIA

DOMAINE ANTOINE-MARIE ARENA

DOMAINE COMTE ABBATUCCI

DOMAINE COMTE PERALDI

DOMAINE DE TORRACCIA

DOMAINE GENTILE

DOMAINE GIUDICELLI

DOMAINE JEAN-BAPTISTE ARENA

DOMAINE L'ENCLOS DES ANGES

DOMAINE LECCIA

DOMAINE ORENGA DE GAFFORY

DOMAINE PIERETTI

DOMAINE SANT ARMETTU

DOMAINE SAPARALE

DOMAINE U STILICCIONU

DOMAINE VACCELLI

DOMAINE VICO

DOMAINE ZURIA

TARRA D'ORASI

TARRA DI SOGNU

YVES LECCIA

JURA

CAVEAU DE BACCHUS–LUCIEN
AVIET & FILS

CELLIER SAINT BENOIT

DOMAINE ANDRÉ ET MIREILLE TISSOT

DOMAINE BERTHET-BONDET

DOMAINE DE LA PINTE

DOMAINE DE LA RENARDIÈRE

DOMAINE DE LA TOURAIZE

DOMAINE DE MONTBOURGEAU

DOMAINE DE PÉLICAN

DOMAINE DES CAVARODES

DOMAINE DES MARNES BLANCHES

DOMAINE FRANÇOIS ROUSSET-MARTIN

DOMAINE JEAN-FRANÇOIS GANEVAT

DOMAINE LABET

DOMAINE MACLE

DOMAINE PHILIPPE BUTIN

DOMAINE PHILIPPE CHATILLON

DOMAINE PHILIPPE VANDELLE

DOMAINE PIGNIER

DOMAINE RENAUD BRUYÈRE & ADELINE
HOUILLON

JACQUES PUFFENEY

LES PIEDS SUR TERRE–VINCENT MOREL

MAISON PIERRE OVERNOY

LANGUEDOC-ROUSSILLON

LANGUEDOC

CLOS MARIE

DOMAINE ALAIN CHABANON

DOMAINE D'AIGUES BELLES

DOMAINE D'AUPILHAC

DOMAINE DE DERNACUEILLETTE

DOMAINE DE L'HORTUS

DOMAINE DE MONTCALMÈS

DOMAINE DU PAS DE L'ESCALETTE

DOMAINE LA CONTE DES FLORIS

DOMAINE LA TERRASSE D'ÉLISE

DOMAINE LÉON BARRAL

DOMAINE LES AURELLES

DOMAINE LES MILLES VIGNES

DOMAINE PEYRE ROSE

HÉRITAGE DU PIC SAINT-LOUP

LES VIGNES OUBLIÉES

MAS CAL DEMOURA

MAS D'ALEZON

MAS DE DAUMAS GASSAC

MAS JULLIEN

PRIEURÉ DE SAINT-JEAN DE BÉBIAN

ROC D'ANGLADE

THIERRY NAVARRE

ROUSSILLON

CAVE L'ÉTOILE

CLOS DU ROUGE GORGE

COUME DEL MAS

DOMAINE DANJOU-BANESSY

DOMAINE DE LA RECTORIE

DOMAINE DE RANCY

DOMAINE DES SCHISTES

DOMAINE GARDIÉS

DOMAINE GAUBY

DOMAINE LA TOUR VIEILLE

DOMAINE LES ENFANTS SAUVAGES

DOMAINE PAUL MEUNIER

DOMAINE VIAL-MAGNÈRES

LE ROC DES ANGES

LE SOULA

MAISON CAZES

MAS AMIEL

OLIVIER PITHON

PAYS DE LA LOIRE

BOURGUEIL, SAINT-NICOLAS-DE-
BOURGUEIL

DOMAINE DE L'OUBLIÉE

DOMAINE DE LA COTELLERAIE

DOMAINE DU BEL AIR

DOMAINE YANNICK AMIRAULT

MAS LA CHEVALIÈRE

STÉPHANE GUION

CHINON

BERNARD BAUDRY

CHARLES JOGUET

CHÂTEAU DE COULAINE

DOMAINE DE LA NOBLAIE

DOMAINE GROSBOIS

PHILIPPE ALLIET

MENETOU-SALON, QUINCAY,
TOURAINE-CHENONCEAUX

DOMAINE MICHAUD

DOMAINE PELLÉ

DOMAINES MINCHIN

LES POËTE

MUSCADET

DOMAINE DE BELLEVUE

DOMAINE DE L'ÉCU

DOMAINE HAUTE FÉVRIE

DOMAINE LUNEAU-PAPIN

DOMAINES LANDRON

SANCERRE AND POUILLY-FUMÉ

ALPHONE MELLOT

DOMAINE A. CAILBOURDIN
DOMAINE DELAPORTE
DOMAINE DIDIER DAGUENEAU
DOMAINE FRANÇOIS COTAT
DOMAINE GÉRARD BOULAY
DOMAINE SERGE DAGUENEAU & FILLES
DOMAINE THOMAS & FILS
DOMAINE VACHERON
DOMAINE VINCENT PINARD
PASCAL ET NICOLAS REVERDY
PAUL PRIEUR & FILS

SAUMUR, SAUMUR-CHAMPIGNY
ARNAUD LAMBERT
CHÂTEAU DE VILLENEUVE
CHÂTEAU DU HUREAU
CHÂTEAU YVONNE
CLOS DE L'ECOTARD
CLOS ROUGEARD
CLOTILDE ET RENÉ-NOËL LEGRAND
DOMAINE ANTOINE SANZAY
DOMAINE DES ROCHES NEUVES
DOMAINE DU COLLIER
MÉLARIC

SAVENNIÈRES, LAYON, ANJOU
CLAU DE NELL
COULÉE DE SERRANT
DOMAINE AUX MOINES
DOMAINE BELARGUS
DOMAINE DE LA BERGERIE
DOMAINE DES BAUMARD
DOMAINE DROST
DOMAINE LAUREAU
DOMAINE OGEREAU
DOMAINE PATRICK BAUDOUIN
LA FERME DE LA SANSONNIÈRE
RICHARD LEROY
TERRA VITA VINUM
THIBAUD BOUDIGNON
THOMAS BATARDIÈRE

VOUVRAY, MONTLOUIS
CLOS NAUDIN
DOMAINE DE LA TAILLE AUX LOUPS
DOMAINE FRANÇOIS CHIDAINE
DOMAINE HUET
DOMAINE SÉBASTIEN BRUNET
VINCENT CARÊME

PROVENCE

BANDOL
CHÂTEAU CROIX D'ALLONS
CHÂTEAU DE PIBARNON

CHÂTEAU PRADEAUX
CHÂTEAU VANNIÈRES
DOMAINE DE LA BÉGUDE
DOMAINE DE LA TOUR DU BON
DOMAINE DE TERREBRUNE
DOMAINE DU GROS' NORÉ
DOMAINE TEMPIER

BAUX-DE-PROVENCE
CHÂTEAU ROMANIN
DOMAINE DE TRÉVALLON
DOMAINE DES TERRES BLANCHES
DOMAINE HAUVETTE
DOMAINE MILAN
MAS DE LA DAME

CASSIS
CLOS SAINTE-MAGDELEINE
DOMAINE DE LA FERME BLANCHE
FONTCREUSE

CÔTE-DE-PROVENCE, BELLET
CHÂTEAU DE MIRAVAL
CHÂTEAU DE ROQUEFORT
CHÂTEAU MALHERBE
CLOS CIBONNE
CLOS SAINT-VINCENT
DOMAINE GAVOTY
DOMAINES OTT
RIMAURESQ

COTEAUX-D'AIX-EN-PROVENCE, PALETTE
CHÂTEAU BAS
CHÂTEAU CALISSANNE
CHÂTEAU HENRI BONNAUD
CHÂTEAU REVELETTE
CHÂTEAU SIMONE
DOMAINE LES BASTIDES
DOMAINE RICHEAUME
VILLA MINNA VINEYARD

SAVOY

CHARLOTTE SONJON
CHÂTEAU DE LA MAR
CORENTIN HOUILLON
DOMAINE ADRIEN BERLIOZ
DOMAINE ANNE-SOPHIE ET JEAN-FRANÇOIS
    QUÉNARD
DOMAINE BÄRTSCHI
DOMAINE CHEVILLARD
DOMAINE DE VALLIER
DOMAINE DES ARDOISIÈRES
DOMAINE DES CÔTES ROUSSES

DOMAINE DES ORCHIS
DOMAINE DU GRINGET
DOMAINE GENOUX
DOMAINE GIACHINO
DOMAINE LE PRIEURE SAINT-HUGHES
DOMAINE LES ARICOQUES
DOMAINE LOUIS MAGNIN
DOMAINE LUDOVIC ARCHER
DOMAINE MASSON
DOMAINE PARTAGE–GILLES BERLIOZ
DOMAINE PASCAL, ANNICK & NOÉ QUENARD
DOMAINE PAUL GADENNE
L'AITONNEMENT
LES FILS DE CHARLES TROSSET
MAISON BONNARD
MAISON GUIGARD
PHILIPPE & SYLVAIN RAVIER

SOUTHWEST

BERGERAC, MONTBAZILLAC
CHÂTEAU TIRECUL LA GRAVIÈRE
CHÂTEAU TOUR DES GENDRES
DOMAINE ALBERT DE CONTI
DOMAINE JULIEN AUROUX

CAHORS
CHÂTEAU DU CÈDRE
CHÂTEAU LAGRÉZETTE
CLOS DE GAMOT
DOMAINE COSSE MAISONNEUVE
DOMAINE LA CALMETTE

CÔTES DU MARMANDAIS
ELIAN DA ROS

GAILLAC, FRONTON
CHÂTEAU BELLEVUE LA FOREST
DOMAINE DE BRIN
DOMAINE PLAGEOLES
DOMAINE PLAISANCE PENAVAYRE
LA COLOMBIÈRE

IROULÉGUY
BORDAXURIA
DOMAINE ARRETXEA
DOMAINE DOMINICA
DOMAINE ETXONDOA
DOMAINE XUBIALDEA
GOIENETXEA
VIGNOBLES BERROUET

JURANÇON
CAMIN LARREDYA
CHARLES HOURS

CLOS JOLIETTE
CLOS LARROUYAT
DOMAINE BRU BACHÉ
DOMAINE CAUHAPÉ
DOMAINE DE SOUCH
LES JARDINS DE BABYLONE

PACHERENC DU VIC-BILH, MADIRAN, SAINT MONT
CHÂTEAU BOUSCASSÉ
CHÂTEAU MONTUS
DOMAINE LABRANCHE LAFFONT
MAS DEL PÉRIÉ
PLAIMONT

RHÔNE VALLEY

CAIRANNE, RASTEAU, BEAUMES-DE-VENISE
DOMAINE DES BERNARDINS
DOMAINE DES ESCARAVAILLES
DOMAINE GOURT DE MAUTENS
DOMAINE LA COLLIÈRE
DOMAINE LA SOUMADE
DOMAINE RICHAUD
DOMAINE ROCHE

CHÂTEAUNEUF-DU-PAPE
CHÂTEAU DE BEAUCASTEL
CHÂTEAU DE LA GARDINE
CHÂTEAU MONT-REDON
CHÂTEAU RAYAS
CLOS DES PAPES
CLOS DU MONT-OLIVET
DOMAINE CHARVIN
DOMAINE DE BEAURENARD
DOMAINE DE CRISTIA
DOMAINE DE LA JANASSE
DOMAINE DE MARCOUX
DOMAINE DURIEU
DOMAINE GIRAUD
DOMAINE JÉRÔME GRADASSI
DOMAINE LA BARROCHE
DOMAINE PIERRE ANDRÉ
DOMAINE PIERRE USSEGLIO
DOMAINE SAINT-PRÉFERT
LE VIEUX DONJON
P. FERRAUD & FILS
VIEUX TÉLÉGRAPHE

CÔTE-DU-RHÔNE, VENTOUX
CHÂTEAU DE FONSALETTE
CHÂTEAU DES TOURS
CHÂTEAU JUVENAL
DOMAINE DAMBRUN
DOMAINE DE GRAMENON

DOMAINE DES GRAVENNES
MARTINELLE
MAS DES VOLQUES

CÔTE-RÔTIE, CONDRIEU
ANDRÉ PERRET
CHÂTEAU GRILLET
DOMAINE BARGE
DOMAINE BURGAUD
DOMAINE CHRISTOPHE SEMASKA
DOMAINE E. GUIGAL
DOMAINE EYMIN-TICHOUX
DOMAINE FRANÇOIS & FILS
DOMAINE GEORGES VERNAY
DOMAINE GERIN
DOMAINE JAMET
DOMAINE JASMIN
DOMAINE MATHILDE ET YVES GANGLOFF
DOMAINE PATRICK ET CHRISTOPHE BONNE-FOND
DOMAINE ROSTAING
MAISON CLUSEL ROCH
PIERRE-JEAN VILLA
STÉPHANE OGIER

CORNAS
DOMAINE AUGUSTE CLAPE
DOMAINE DU COULET
DOMAINE DU TUNNEL
DOMAINE ÉRIC ET JOËL DURAND
DOMAINE FRANCK BALTHAZAR
DOMAINE LIONNET
DOMAINE VINCENT PARIS
THIERRY ALLEMAND

GIGONDAS AND VACQUEYRAS
DOMAINE D'OURÉA
DOMAINE DES BOSQUETS
DOMAINE LA BOUÏSSIÈRE
DOMAINE LE SANG DES CAILLOUX
DOMAINE RASPAIL-AY
DOMAINE SANTA DUC

HERMITAGE, CROZES-HERMITAGE
BERNARD FAURIE
CAVE DE TAIN
DOMAINE ALAIN GRAILLOT
DOMAINE CHAMBEYRON
DOMAINE COMBIER
DOMAINE DU COLOMBIER
DOMAINE EMMANUEL DARNAUD
DOMAINE JEAN-LOUIS CHAVE
DOMAINE LES BRUYÈRES
DOMAINE MARC SORREL
DOMAINE PAUL JABOULET AÎNÉ
M. CHAPOUTIER
YANN CHAVE

SAINT-JOSEPH
DOMAINE AURÉLIEN CHATAGNIER
DOMAINE BERNARD GRIPA
DOMAINE DU MONTEILLET–STÉPHANE MONTEZ
DOMAINE GONON
DOMAINE MARSANNE
MAISON LOUIS CHÈZE

TAVEL
CHÂTEAU D'AQUERIA
CHÂTEAU TRINQUEVEDEL
DOMAINE DE LA MORDORÉE

ACKNOWLEDGMENTS

To all the winegrowers who have welcomed me with passion, modesty, and a generous spirit. Thank you for your time, your stories, your wines, and your vineyards, which you enrich through the respect you express in everything you do.

To Mary Bernardo, my sister and great companion, with whom I often share travels through the world of wine, for lightheartedness, high spirits, and a lust for life.

To Bruno Tessarech, the friend who, thanks to his empathy and sensitivity, ensures the quality of my prose, bringing depth, nobility, and a philosophical spirit to the grand journey that is writing.

To all the many friends with whom I so often have the pleasure of sharing a fine glass of champagne.

To Prosper, Martine, and the entire team at Assouline Publishing, who have allowed me to express myself with heart and professionalism.

To my parents, my sisters, and my brother, my only certitudes in a world that keeps me moving forward when in doubt.

A cheese, bread and wine composition photographed by James Beck, in 2020.

ABOUT THE AUTHOR

Enrico Bernardo made his name at Le V, the restaurant at the Four Seasons George V in Paris, and was named Best Sommelier of the World in 2004. As a restaurateur, he has created and owned several Michelin star–holding restaurants, focused on pairing the perfect wine with each dish. Bernardo consults for food, wine and art de vivre companies worldwide and is the author of several books including *The Impossible Collection of Wine* (2016), *La Sagesse du Vin* (2021) and *The Impossible Collection of Champagne* (2022). In 2018, he undertook a world wine trip, broadening his knowledge of the industry and bringing unknown talents to light.

CREDITS:

ONE TREE PLANTED

Assouline supports *One Tree Planted*
in its commitment to create a more
sustainable world through reforestation.

Front cover design: © Assouline
Back cover tip-on (clockwise from top left): © Benoît Guenot;
© Benoît Guenot; © Philippe Pascal; © Gilbert Bages
Endpages: Design © Assouline
Regional Maps: © Thibault Bouisset
Map of France (p.4): © Valeria Ramírez Reyes

© 2024 Assouline Publishing
3 Park Avenue, 27th floor
New York, NY 10016 USA
Tel: 212-989-6769 Fax: 212-647-0005
assouline.com

Editor: Léana Esch
Art Director: Sébastien Ratto-Viviani
Designer: Florence Reynier
Photo editor: Muse Giacalone

Printed in Italy by Grafiche Milani, on Fedrigoni
Symbol Freelife paper, produced in Italy under the
strictest environmental standards.
ISBN: 9781649803849
10 9 8 7 6 5 4 3 2

MIX
Paper | Supporting
responsible forestry
FSC® C021849

Produit de France

Mis en bouteilles à la propriété

Montrachet
GRAND CRU
APPELLATION MONTRACHET CONTRÔLÉE

DOMAINE LEFLAIVE
PROPRIÉTAIRE A PULIGNY-MONTRACHET (CÔTE-D'OR)

MIS EN BOUTEILLE AU CHÂTEAU

CHATEAU LAFITE-ROTHSCHILD
1982
PAUILLAC
APPELLATION PAUILLAC CONTRÔLÉE

PRODUCE OF FRANCE 75cl

DÉPOSÉ SOCIÉTÉ CIVILE DU CHÂTEAU LAFITE-ROTHSCHILD, PROPRIÉTAIRE A PAUILLAC (GIRONDE)

GRAND VIN
DE
CHATEAU LATOUR
PREMIER GRAND CRU CLASSÉ
APPELLATION PAUILLAC CONTRÔLÉE
PAUILLAC-MÉDOC
1961
MIS EN BOUTEILLES AU CHATEAU

MONTRACHET
GRAND CRU
APPELLATION MONTRACHET GRAND CRU CONTRÔLÉE
1992
DOMAINE DES COMTES LAFON

Mis en bouteilles à la Propriété

CLOS DE LA BARRE
21190 MEURSAULT
FRANCE

Produit de France 75 cl.

ALSACE
APPELLATION ALSACE CONTRÔLÉE

Clos Ste Hune
RIESLING 750 ml

A RIBEAUVILLÉ & HUNAWIHR FRANCE
S SULFITES PRODUIT DE FRANCE

GRAND VIN DE LÉOVILLE
du Marquis de LAS CASES
Appellation Saint-Julien Contrôlée
PROPRE SOCIÉTÉ CIVILE DU CHATEAU LÉOVILLE, LAS CASES A SAINT-JULIEN (Gde)
MIS EN BOUTEILLES
AU CHATEAU RECOLTE 1959

15% alc/vol.

CHÂ
APP
S.C.E.H. DU CLOS P
à CHATEAU
MIS EN BOUTEILLE A L

Château d'Y
Lur-Salud

CHÂTEAU
LA MISSION HAUT BRION
Grand Premier Cru
1929

MIS EN Bouteilles au Château
BORDEAUX

LA T
APPELLATION LA T
17.137 Boutee
BOUTEILLE Nº
ANNÉE 1991

Mise en boutei

E. GUIGAL
CÔTE-RÔTIE
APPELLATION CÔTE-RÔTIE CONTRÔLÉE
PRODUIT DE FRANCE

ANGELUS
GRAND CRU CLASSÉ
CHATEAU
ANGELUS
1989
St Emilion Grand Cru
DE BOÜARD DE LAFOREST & FILS
PROPRIÉTAIRES A SAINT-EMILION - FRANCE
Appellation St-Emilion Grand Cru Contrôlée
13,5% vol. 75 cl.
PRODUCE OF FRANCE
MIS EN BOUTEILLE AU CHATEAU

ROMANÉE-CONTI
APPELLATION ROMANÉE-CONTI CONTRÔLÉE

7.446 Bouteilles Récoltées

BOUTEILLE Nº
ANNÉE 1990

LES ASSOCIÉS-GÉ
ChadesRoc
A. de

Mise en bouteille au domaine

PRODUCE OF FRANCE

Extra Quality
Very Dry

CHAMPAG

Renaudin, Bollinger & Co.,
Ay-Champagne.
1924 Vintage.

MARGAUX CHATE

MIS EN BOU
SOCIÉTÉ CIVILE DU

1945
ANNÉE DE LA VICTOIRE

1945
Cette récolte a produit
24 jéroboams numérotés de A à Y
1475 magnums numér.de M à M.1475
74422 bouts.½ bout.numér.de 1 à 74422
2000 Réserve du Château marqués R E
Cette bouteille porte le Nº R.C.

Château
Mouton Rothschild
APPELLATION PAUILLAC CONTRÔLÉE

GRAND CRU
RICHEBOURG
APPELLATION RICHEBOURG CONTRÔLÉE

Domaine Méo-Camuzet
PROPRIÉTAIRE A VOSNE-ROMANÉE, BOURGOGNE, FRANCE
ALC. 12.5% BY VOL. - PRODUCE OF FRANCE - RED BURGUNDY WINE - 750ML

Clos de Tart
GRAND CRU
MONOPOLE

VOSNE-
CLOS DU
MO

MIS EN BOUT
DOMAINE DU VIC
VIGNERON AU CHÂT

28

SEC

Réserve
Nº 00186

Henri Jayer
Production
800 bouteilles

VOSNE - ROMANÉE
APPELLATION VOSNE-ROMANÉE CONTRÔLÉE
CROS-PARANTOUX

Mis en bouteille par
Henri Jayer

PRODUIT DE FRANCE VIN

Cornas
APPELLATION CORNAS CONTRÔLÉE
RHÔNE WINE
MIS EN BOUTEILLE À LA PROPRIÉTÉ
DOMAINE A. CLAPE, SCEA
PROPRIÉTAIRE-VITICULTEUR À CORNAS (ARDÈCHE)

ALC. 13 % BY VOL. 750 ML

PRODUCT OF FRANCE WINE

CHATEAU HAUT-BRION
CRU CLASSÉ DES GRAVES
Pessac-Léognan
Appellation Pessac-Léognan Contrôlée
Premier Grand Cru Classé en 1855
Mis en bouteille au Château
Domaine Clarence Dillon s.a. propriétaire, Pessac, Gironde, F 33600

13,5% vol 75 cl
L HBR 00 D

Mus
GRAN
APPELLATION
RED BURGUND

Domaine
PROPRIÉTAIRE A CHAMBOLLE-M

19

Vins de

CARI